W9-BGV-443

LIVE, LOVE, EXPLORE

Praise for *Live, Love, Explore*

"It took me at least ten years to understand the connection between my travels and the life lessons that got me through tough times. *Live, Love, Explore* gets you there quicker to celebrate the wonderful, frightening, unexpected journey of life."

—Samantha Brown, world traveler and Travel Channel TV host

"*Live, Love, Explore* is a bona fide page-turner—full of inspiring personal stories, charming anecdotes, and thought-provoking questions. You won't want to put it down!"

—Light Watkins, founder of the Shine Movement

"*Live, Love, Explore* is a must-read for anyone searching for their true purpose in life. Inspiring and insightful, it outlines the lessons of the Way of the Traveler, a way of life to which we can all aspire."

—Mark Divine, Commander, US Navy SEALs (retired), founder of SEALFIT, and bestselling author of *The Way of the SEAL*

"*Live, Love, Explore* is an instant classic. It reminds all of us that the big dreams we have in our hearts are within reach."

—Shane Jeremy James, founder of Actions of Compassion

"Leon has nailed it. It's rare that one so young 'gets' what we all eventually find out; that the grandest and most difficult of journeys is to find and make peace with ourselves. He not only speaks so eloquently of it, he shows us the way."

—Ted Klontz, coauthor of *The Financial Wisdom of Ebenezer Scrooge*

"*Live, Love, Explore* deserves my highest high kick! Leon's book has helped me find the adventure in my crazy life and can help you, too!"

—Fredrik Eklund, star of BRAVO's *Million Dollar Listing New York* and bestselling author of *The Sell*

"The life I was meant to live has always revolved around travel and media. To read real tips from Leon Logothetis, one of the travel industry's most inspiring figures, made me move beyond the mundane and dream of magical moments and big dreams."

—Annie Fitzsimmons, editor-at-large, *National Geographic Traveler*

"Once Leon Logothetis quit following someone else's path, a brilliant new calling emerged. He discovered the bliss that lies within each of us but is often ignored. Leon shares wonderful real-life experiences that are bound to rejuvenate your soul—often from the most unlikely people and places. *Live, Love, Explore* is entertaining, insightful, and inspiring."

—J.P. Hansen, success coach, inspirational speaker, and bestselling, award-winning author of *The Bliss List* and *Find Your Bliss*

"Leon does it again! In his newest book, Leon so generously shares his experiences which have provided me invaluable guidance on living my best life."

—Brad Jamison, founder of Good Citizen

"In Leon's latest book, the reader is taken on yet another journey of self-exploration and enlightenment. Leon truly represents the nomadic soul of a traveler seeking answers."

—Dane Steele Green, CEO, Steele Luxury Travel, Huffington Post blogger

"*Live, Love, Explore* will introduce you to a world of profound teachings and amazing adventures. Leon weaves a powerful story that will touch your heart long after you have turned the last page. A truly inspiring read!"

—Scott Flansburg, bestselling author of *Turn On the Human Calculator in You*

"In *Live, Love, Explore*, Leon shares his hilarious and heartwarming stores of his adventures on the road. Through his wonderful gift of story, I've learned to live my life more fully and without regrets. Thank you!"

—Lyss Stern, founder and CEO, Divalysscious Moms, bestselling author and columnist

"*Live, Love, Explore* is a kind of beacon for the traveler in all of us. Even if you never leave the comfort of your own home, you'll find that Leon's lessons from the road provide you a treasure map to a better life."

—Oliver Bennett, travel writer for *The Guardian*, *The Times*, *The Telegraph*, and *The Independent*

"Leon sets himself apart with his powerful message paired with such authentic delivery. His insights from his personal experiences have helped me have a more clear vision for a more happy and fulfilling life. *Live, Love, Explore* is funny, deeply moving and beyond inspiring."

—Margie Warrell, life coach and bestselling author of *Brave*

LIVE

DISCOVER THE WAY OF THE TRAVELER

LOVE

A ROAD MAP TO THE LIFE YOU WERE MEANT TO LIVE

EXPLORE

LEON LOGOTHETIS

Reader's
digest

NEW YORK • MONTREAL

A READER'S DIGEST BOOK

Copyright © 2017 Winston Enterprises, LLC

All rights reserved. Unauthorized reproduction, in any manner, is prohibited.

Reader's Digest is a registered trademark of Trusted Media Brands, Inc.

Photo on page xii courtesy of the author.

This is a true story and the characters and events are real. Some of the names have been changed, and some material has been altered, combined, or condensed for narrative clarity, but the overall chronology is an accurate depiction of the author's experience.

Library of Congress Cataloging-in-Publication Data
Names: Logothetis, Leon, author.
Title: Live, love, explore : discover the way of the traveler : a road map to
    the life you were meant to live / Leon Logothetis.
Description: New York, NY ; Montreal : Readers Digest, Trusted Media Brands, Inc.,
    [2016]
Identifiers: LCCN 2016018324 | ISBN 9781621453239 (hardcover) | ISBN
9781621453383 (paperback) | ISBN 9781621453246 (epub)
Subjects: LCSH: Conduct of life. | Life.
Classification: LCC BJ1589 .L64 2016 | DDC 158.1--dc23 LC record available at
https://lccn.loc.gov/2016018324

We are committed to both the quality of our products and the service we provide to our customers. We value your comments, so please feel free to contact us.
Reader's Digest Trade Publishing
44 South Broadway
White Plains, NY 10601

For more Reader's Digest products and information, visit our website:
www.rd.com (in the United States)
www.readersdigest.ca (in Canada)

Printed in China

10 9 8 7 6 5 4 3 2 1 (hardcover)
10 9 8 7 6 5 4 3 2 1 (paperback)

George, Con, and Nick
One for all and all for one

"We must be willing to get rid of the life we've planned so as to have the life that is waiting for us."

—JOSEPH CAMPBELL

"The key to immortality is first living a life worth remembering."

—BRUCE LEE

CONTENTS

LIVE, LOVE, EXPLORE

INTRODUCTION

MY WAY INTO THE WORLD

"We travel, initially, to lose ourselves; and we travel, next, to find ourselves."

—PICO IYER

I was tired of living someone else's life.

Since childhood, I had been told what to do, how to act, who to be. I had been instructed through other people's expectations, their demands, even their unspoken judgment, that the only way to be happy was to become a carbon copy of the people around me. And for many years, I was okay following in their footsteps. I was okay showing up to my office job, wearing the suit, playing the role, but that was the thing: I was playing a role. I wasn't actually being my truest self.

I was tired of living someone else's life. I wanted to live my own. And I wanted my life to be amazing. I wanted it to be filled with adventure. I wanted to live with such unbridled passion that every bit of food would taste richer, every inch of sky would be brighter, every breath of air more alive.

Which is how I ended up in Nepal.

It was a haphazard trip, really. I went there with only my plane ticket, a backpack, and the quiet, desperate knowledge that my life had to change.

Something did. For two weeks, I followed a guide through barren landscapes, along treacherous mountain passes, through bustling cities, and crowded slums. I met strangers on buses, and fell in love with every face that greeted me along the way. And I never wanted to leave.

On one of my last mornings in that magnificent land, I woke up to watch the sunrise. I stood out on a balcony overlooking Kathmandu, and as though to announce the beginning of a new life, an eagle flew overhead, calling out in the morning fog, calling out to me. It felt as though I were looking out across the whole of the world—filled with billions of lives and stories waiting to be heard, and adventures waiting to be lived. I wanted to meet every one of them. I wanted to honor their stories. I wanted to live and breathe and embrace adventure in such a way that it would become a part of my DNA, a thread so embedded in my life, I could never again exist without it. And there, on that balcony, on that fateful morning, I began to discover what it meant to live the Way of the Traveler.

During that trip through Nepal, I discovered that the world held more than just landmarks. It held lifetimes of wisdom and centuries of dreams, both fulfilled and unfulfilled. Standing there, looking out at that magnificent sunrise, the eagle soaring ahead just as the first light of day crested the horizon, I realized that for once, I was finally living my dream. For once, I was authentically, brazenly alive.

I had dragged along a copy of *Moby-Dick* because books have often been the great stimuli of my adventures, igniting my curiosity and driving me out into the world. At that point in my life, I felt like I was hunting my own white whale: I was searching for my purpose.

The day after I landed in Nepal, I met Aardash, a guide who offered to take me across Nepal for a nominal fee. Aardash was about a foot shorter than I am, with thick arms and legs, and a dark bowl of heavy hair. We were nearly the same age, but while I walked like a man who didn't know where he was going (because at twenty-two, I really didn't), Aardash had a strong and easy gait, matching a demeanor that calmly accepted every twist in our tumultuous road.

Though at first most of Aardash's words had centered on telling me when to stop and when to go ("We walk now," was his most frequent command), we soon found a rhythm to our relationship. Over two weeks, we had trekked across Nepal, until the morning when I ended up on that balcony overlooking the world.

As Ishmael says in *Moby-Dick*, "Whenever I find myself growing grim about the mouth; whenever it is a damp, drizzly November in my soul . . . then, I account it high time to get to sea as soon as I can."

Call me Leon.

Call me the traveler.

Call me the accidental teacher, who took a walk through Nepal, and ended up seeing the whole of the world.

What I found there—and what I have found in the nearly ninety countries I have visited since—is that we are all looking for the same thing. No matter who we are or where we live or what sort of travails befall us, we all want to be seen and heard and loved. We all crave connection, and we are all inspired by the greatest adventure of all: finding the life we were meant to live.

So, what is the Way of the Traveler, you ask? It's simple, my friends. The Way of the Traveler is a state of being. It is a road map to living your best life, to loving with all your heart, to exploring the world around you, and even more importantly, to exploring the world within yourself.

The Way of the Traveler teaches us how to live with unbridled passion—the type that makes food richer, the sky brighter, and yes, every breath of air more alive. It is a movement. It is a way of life. And ultimately, it's about being fully present in every moment, in every choice, in every thought and feeling, so we never again end up playing a role. It demands that we walk away from old ideas, and instead walk in the direction of our dreams. And it shows us how to dance more deeply with ourselves so we may dance more frequently with one another.

The law of inertia dictates that the first few movements toward change are always met with the most resistance, but that doesn't mean we aren't capable of change. In fact, we *have* to change. We have to grow. We have to challenge ourselves, or we will—spiritually, emotionally, or even physically—die.

The Way of the Traveler is a different path for everyone. We don't all meet at the same destination, and we certainly take different routes. Because the Way of the Traveler doesn't occur only on Nepalese hillsides. It takes place in the darkest reaches of our souls, when we view the landscape within ourselves. It occurs in the worlds we inhabit every day without even leaving our homes, and the ones around us—with our friends and family, in the communities where we live, the world we see in the news, and the world we can feel all around us.

Like the great Muhammad Ali once said "Me. We." Because once we take down the barriers between the lives we're living now and the ones we were meant to live, down come the barriers between us and everyone else. We look at the whole world expanding around us, and suddenly it is not a remote and foreign landscape. It lines the walls of our souls. But more than that, if I see you, truly *see* you, with clear eyes and an open heart, then guess what? I finally get to see me, too. All those layers of ambition and fear and loneliness and doubt and boredom fall away, and we become our truest selves. We will awaken on that first sunrise, transformed by a dawn that stands out from all the others.

So Aardash. And Nepal. And that sunrise I keep talking about.

Aardash and I walked twenty to thirty miles each day, hitch-hiking when we could find a ride, hopping trains when we stumbled upon a station. We slept where we could. We made up stupid songs and laughed along the train tracks. And out on those roads—which at times were overflowing with buses and trucks and people, at other times as barren as the stark mountains around them—I felt at home in ways I had never felt before.

I didn't know where we were going, but for the first time in my life I was okay with being led. I had spent my whole life demanding things from life, without realizing that what I asked for was rarely what I wanted. And then, suddenly, with my new Nepalese friend calling all the shots, I was beginning to feel something shift. I wasn't sure what yet, but that movement toward change was beginning to be met with less resistance.

Scientists have proven that our minds' neural networks are shaped by the relationships in our lives. We are neurologically altered by our connections to others. Though I didn't quite understand it on that trip, my relationship with Aardash was changing everything inside me. It was changing the way I saw the world. It was changing what I wanted my *own* world to look like, painting it in different colors and in a myriad of different possibilities. Suddenly, spending my life behind a desk didn't seem like the only option. My great white whale was beginning to surface above water, my purpose suddenly rising up to greet me—this adventurous path of travel was my road. It was where I belonged, where I felt most connected to myself and the world around me. And I needed to keep walking along it.

On our last night, Aardash and I made it back to Kathmandu, just in time for my flight the next day.

"If you wish," he offered, "we eat and stay with my family."

He might as well have offered a night at the Taj Mahal.

"I would be honored," was my honest reply.

That night, I had dinner in the small apartment where Aardash lived with his brother, his brother's wife, and their three children. That next and final morning, I walked out onto the balcony of Aardash's home, overlooking the city and slums, the crystalline mountains breaking through the smog of the city. I knew it was time to stop delaying my dreams. It was time to set sail on the open and treacherous seas of the world every day.

I breathed in the air, and I knew this was what I was meant to do. I belonged out here in the world. I wanted to be taught by every Aardash in every city and empty canyon I could find. And I wanted to share those teachings with anyone who would listen.

So I'm glad you're listening.

That was the first morning of the Way of the Traveler. The morning I decided I would stop living the life that was shaped for me by others, and start living the life I had always dreamed of creating. But did I go home, quit my job, and change my life forever? Not right away, because sometimes epiphanies occur at slow burn. Over the next few years, I would come to understand that "Me. We." actually takes place everywhere—at home, in our communities, in our work. It happens every time we connect with another person. It happens when we connect with those we love most. It happens when we find a group of similarly searching sailors, and we go out into the world, not entirely sure of our destination, but knowing that it will certainly be worth the adventure.

As Ishmael says in *Moby-Dick*, "It is not down in any map; true places never are."

I have found we're not always aware when we are arriving at those "true" places. Sometimes I have had life-changing adventures or experiences that in the moment felt like anything but. Similarly, the stories I am about to share don't take place in any sort of linear chronological fashion. Over the last fifteen years, the Way of the Traveler has slowly revealed itself. At times, I had no idea I was on its path; at others, I was keenly aware. And there are times, even now, when I am forced to recognize that I still haven't figured it out.

Because the Way of the Traveler is not ultimately about what we find, it is about the journey we take to get there. And like you, I am still very much on that journey. I am far from perfect, and as I think you'll realize pretty quickly, I can still be fairly screwed up. But the Way of the Traveler has shown me that imperfect teachers are sometimes the most powerful. We don't learn when the trains run on time. We learn when we're being derailed.

My personal journeys have introduced me to hundreds of different teachers, some of whom I will introduce to you. You will meet the pimp from New Jersey who taught me about taking risks. You will join me as I drive a London taxicab across America and, in the process, learn how to let go. And you will meet the guru whom I followed through India in search of myself. I'm still searching, but that's also part of being a traveler. The adventure never ends; it's in the seeking that real change takes place.

I will forewarn you right now, the Way of the Traveler demands that we take action. You cannot find your purpose simply by reading this book.

Because the Way of the Traveler begs us to go within, to ask the hard questions, to discover the deep truths. Some of those truths might require that we change our lives. And others might show us that sometimes what we have right in front of us is all we ever needed in the first place.

If you're looking for more than what you find here, you can go to WayoftheTraveler.com, where you will have opportunities to watch videos, participate in exercises, and become a part of a community of fellow travelers. Either way, I hope that you are willing to do the work, and that you begin that work today with this book.

You will discover words of encouragement scattered throughout the following pages, like handwritten signs along the path. They will be as much a part of your journey as the rest of the text, as these sentences are actually affirmations—statements that you can and should make to yourself every morning. You may want to write your favorites down, the ones that really speak to you, and choose to start each day with one.

You can say them out loud if you're feeling bold, or you can read them to yourself until you begin to feel bold. But allow them to guide each day as you journey along the Way of the Traveler.

This voyage doesn't require that you go anywhere, except within yourself. But that adventure is quite possibly the greatest and most terrifying one of all. It demands that you ask for direction, that you face whatever obstacles lie in your path, and that you are willing to alter your destination as you learn more about yourself. It insists that you recognize who and what you are inviting into your life. Are you living with despair and loneliness? Are you making choices based not on who you are but on who others think you should be? Are you trapped in the idea that only a few select people are allowed to realize their dreams, and the rest of us must simply clock in until the day we clock out? Are you tired of regretting not jumping off that high dive, the wind rushing past, the cold plunge of water reminding you, that for today, in this moment, you are brilliantly, madly alive?

I am asking you to join me on that adventurous road. Through every trip I share in this book, I will ask you to participate in a variety of exercises, where you will have the opportunity take your own adventure, whether it is into the relationships in your life, the community where you live, or perhaps the most dangerous journey of all, into the deepest reaches of your soul. You will come to understand who you really are, who you were always meant to be. At the end of it, will you quit your job and start traveling the globe? Not necessarily.

But I suspect you will learn what the Way of the Traveler has taught me: The adventure always, always lies within.

So here we go. Get your backpack ready, your water bottle filled. I promise that, at the end of this book, you will walk out and see the sunrise, and I hope you, too, will see in its dawning daylight the truths that for too long have been covered by the fog of boredom and the pollution of fear. I hope that you begin to doubt everything, and that in turn, you begin to trust the world.

Are you ready? I know I am. As Aardash said to me on that morning when he found me on the balcony overlooking the world, "We walk now?"

Me. We. We walk now.

ONE

TAKING RISKS
IS THE ONLY WAY

"The person who risks nothing, does nothing, has nothing, is nothing, and becomes nothing. He may avoid suffering and sorrow, but he simply cannot learn and feel and change and grow and love and live."

—LEO F. BUSCAGLIA

There is no greater magic than childhood. Even for those whose early years were difficult or traumatic, the miracles of growing up shine within us all—because one of the great aspects of childhood is that every day is filled with wonder.

Most of us spend our childhoods dreaming and hoping, plotting for what our wondrous adulthoods might hold. We build forts and call them castles. We run through the backyards of our friends being chased by dragons in the woods. We are heroes and princesses and kings and unicorns and soldiers

13

and mermaids and astronauts and firefighters and rock stars and soaring birds. And we believe that one day, we will grow up to be whatever we dream of being.

What if I said we weren't wrong?

What if I told you that you could still be a hero or a princess or a king or even a freaking unicorn?

Now, I've been accused of being crazy before, but hear me out. The only thing that stops us from being whatever we dream of being is us.

Which means the only person who can help us to be whatever we dream of being is also us. And that is the great miracle of adulthood.

The writer Joseph Campbell once told a great story about overhearing a couple with their child in a restaurant. The father said to the boy, "Drink your tomato juice." And the boy said, "I don't want to." His mother then jumped in, defending the child, "Don't make him do what he doesn't want to do." To which the father replied, as fathers have replied for centuries, "He can't go through life doing what he wants to do. If he does only what he wants to do, he'll be dead."

Where is your inner child?

Far too often, children are raised with the same message. We began to believe that we couldn't go through life doing what we wanted to do. We were sure that doing so would only lead to certain death. So instead, we lived in fear. We learned to weigh the risks of our lives, to limit our dreams to the expectations and demands of others. But here's the thing: You can't go anywhere in life without taking a risk. And the only person whose approval is really worth something is your own.

In June of 1876, the U.S. Army and several Native American tribes fought the Battle of the Little Big Horn, known to most as Custer's Last Stand. It was a terribly bloody dispute, but as it was nearing its close, the tribes made their final push toward victory, running directly into gunfire as one of them called out, "Today is a good day to die!"

Now, I am not advocating that you engage in a massive land battle, but I am advocating that you start jumping into your life. That you start taking risks, because you don't have to drink the tomato juice if you don't want to. And there's still time for all of us to become unicorns. The Way of the Traveler has shown me that the only way back to that magic of childhood, that great joy of fearlessness, is by taking risks.

The minute we decide to do something different, we open up a world of fear and uncertainty—but we also find the path where we will finally discover who we truly are. I was introduced to that path on a rainy evening in London, which at that time had been my only home for all of my young life.

If you have ever read anything written by me, or seen any show or any blog that I've been a part of, then you know my whole life shifted one quiet night at home, watching *The Motorcycle Diaries*. A movie based on the life of Che Guevara, it tells the story of him riding a motorcycle across South America, living with strangers and meeting the world. I had just turned twenty-seven. I was working as a broker. I was wondering why I had failed to keep the promises I had made to myself on that eye-opening trip to Nepal, which had taken place a few years earlier. (As I said, the Way of the Traveler is not necessarily a linear journey.)

Sitting in my living room in London, exhausted by another day at the office, I had no idea that watching a movie would change my life as much as backpacking through Nepal, but inspiration has many sources. And that night, lying on my living room couch, I knew—just as I had known while looking out from that balcony in Kathmandu—that it was time for me to take another step on the Way of the Traveler, to make a bold and wild movement toward change.

THE PUZZLE PIECES

Not all risk involves changing *everything* in your life. Sometimes all it takes is making one small tweak to get us where we need to be. But first we have to figure out how we got where we are.

When I was fifteen years old, I had my heart broken for the first time. I had fallen in love with my best friend's neighbor. She was beautiful and smart and had long, red, wavy hair and a dimple in her left cheek. I wanted her to know how much I loved her, but I was too terrified to say anything.

Like many a Romeo before me, I decided that I would give

her a token of my admiration. After taking stock of everything in our house, I decided to give her a little China plate
that my aunt had given me. I thought that once my beloved
received this finely engraved piece of dinnerware, she would
certainly fall in love with me, and all would be right with the
world.

That did not happen. In fact, according to my best friend,
who was our intermediary, she thought I was weird.

For years, that story echoed through my life. It was one of
the many pieces of evidence I had collected that being vulnerable just hurt too much. Love clearly demanded heartbreak, and
I wasn't sure I could handle that.

In *The Drama of the Gifted Child*, renowned psychologist
Alice Miller explains that our greatest tool is "the emotional
discovery of the truth about the unique history of our childhood." Many of us have sat at that restaurant table with our
parents. We were told we had to listen or else we might die,
and yet we knew that was a lie. Growing up, I was called weird
and different, so when I grew up I worked desperately to be
like everyone else. I worked to forget the dreams that once populated my childhood—the stories of knights and astronauts
and great travelers who sailed the seven seas and saved maidens
along the way. But I didn't just lose the dreams of childhood. I
also lost the magic of fearless wonder. I worried so much about
what other people thought of me that I could never actually be
myself.

I wasn't funny. I wasn't even particularly pleasant. I allowed fear to seep into every belief I held and every choice I made. And I allowed it to stop me from following my dreams. In the moment though, I didn't call it fear. I thought I was just too busy . . . or too lazy. Often, we create lives—choosing professions, spouses, homes—that cater to fear. We fear that we can't live too big, that we don't deserve too much. We fear taking big risks; we fear dreaming big dreams; and in the end, we end up drinking tomato juice for the rest of our lives, when we really wanted orange juice.

Master the fear.

If we look back at our lives with a clear perspective, refusing to allow the excuses we have used for so long to cloud our picture, we begin to see that so many of our choices weren't rooted in passion or purpose. They were rooted in the fear that we didn't have other choices, or the fear that we weren't capable or worthy of anything more.

After watching the story of Che Guevara and his years on the road, I began to look back at my life. I could start to see all the puzzle pieces fall into place. Why had I made the decisions I had made? Because they were easy. Because they were what my family wanted. Because they were the same decisions being made by my friends and the people with whom I grew up. Because I was insecure, always trying to please the people around me, because being myself would make me risk losing their approval. Because being myself would have threatened the belief that making money and working all day and wearing the right clothes and dating the right kind of woman would guarantee me happiness. But what I had discovered in Nepal, what I recognized on Che's journey, was that pleasing the people around me would never bring me joy.

In order to determine where I wanted to go, where my great adventures would take me, I knew that first I needed to embrace the unique history of my childhood. I had to discover the truth of who I really was. Now, it's time for you to do the same.

What Are Your Key Life Events?

As you look at your own life, what are the five key events that have made you who you are today, either connecting you to your sense of purpose or preventing you from realizing it? Think back to your early childhood, and review the challenges of adolescence. Maybe some of these moments took place in your early years of work, marriage, or child-rearing. What five life events have shaped you?

1. _____

_____

_____

_____

_____

2. _____

_____

_____

_____

_____

3. _____

_____

_____

_____

_____

4. _____

_____

_____

_____

_____

5. _____

_____

_____

_____

_____

If I were looking at my own list of key moments, I would include that trip to Nepal as an experience that showed me who
I wanted to be. I would remember back to the night I watched

The Motorcycle Diaries on my couch in London. I would include the day that my best friend's neighbor broke my heart. I would add the day I began to travel the world, relying on the kindness of strangers. And I would include the day my best friend and greatest love, my dog Winnie, died (more on that later).

What's your why?

I would sit down and look at the list, just as I now invite you to do. Think about what the moments on your list have in common. How have they shaped your life? How have they made you grow?

YOUR CREATIVE DNA

In her book *The Creative Habit*, choreographer Twyla Tharp describes what she calls our creative DNA: "I believe that we all have strands of *creative code* hard-wired into our imaginations. These strands are as solidly imprinted in us as the genetic code that determines our height and eye color, except they govern our creative impulses."

We all have this DNA—these strands of creative code that drive us, both toward our dreams or away from them. Those months after seeing *The Motorcycle Diaries* were some of the most painful of my life. I had envisioned the life I was supposed to be living, but I wasn't quite sure what that meant. I mean, really, was I just going to go on vacation for the rest of my life? Financially, that was impossible, but even more than that, it sounded boring. Was I supposed to become a guide in Kathmandu and lead people through Nepal? Though enticing, I knew that by week three, I would have been heading for the Himalayas. So I decided to call the one person who would understand. I called my mum.

I explained my situation, only to hear silence on the other end. I thought she would surely tell me to stay with my job, play it safe. Instead, she asked me the one question I had been avoiding all my life, "What do you want to do?"

After I hung up the phone, I knew what I wanted to do. I wanted to see the world, but I wanted to do so in a way that would force me to engage with it. Not as a tourist, but as part of every city I visited, every community I encountered. I didn't want to go on vacation. I wanted to connect with the world in a way that made me vulnerable, in ways that I knew would surely break my heart. And I also knew that I would never again be able to return to my old life if I didn't at least give it a try.

So now I ask you the same thing. What do you want to do? Look back at those puzzle pieces, those life-shaping stories. Do you see any themes running through them? As I looked at my own, I began to see that my most life-altering moments had occurred when I had made myself vulnerable to the world, like when I handed people the small China plate of my love, whether or not they returned the favor, whether or not they broke my heart. When I thought of my time with

Aardash, my spirit soared like that eagle I saw my last morning in Nepal. It wasn't that I just wanted to see the world. I wanted to meet its people. I wanted to give the whole world a small China plate.

Suddenly, a pattern began to emerge from my puzzle pieces: travel, connection, adventure. They weren't choices being made for me; rather, they were the ones I wanted to make for myself. They were scary. They were downright terrifying. But I also knew that I had to discover that same bravery that the Native Americans displayed, running across the plains. I needed to live each day with the passion of my last. Because, for all we know, this is the only chance we've got.

Embody it all.

What Makes Up Your Creative DNA?

As you look back at your puzzle pieces, what makes up your creative DNA? Your themes might be rooted in creativity: being a writer or actor or sculptor. For others, the themes might have to do with science or math or engineering. For me, it was travel and connectivity and being of service. Determine the three themes that run through your life, and then write down how you can begin dedicating more time to them.

1. _____

_____

_____

_____

_____

2. _____

_____

_____

_____

3. _____

_____

_____

_____

THE BIG DREAM

After my epiphany, I met with my father, and told him I wanted to leave London and travel the world . . . and that I was leaving my job as a broker.

"I know you say you're following your dreams, Leon," he replied, trying to convince me nicely. "But it just sounds like you're trying to avoid your responsibilities."

He wouldn't be the last person to accuse me of that. But

here is one of the first lessons I learned from the road: *Adventure and responsibility aren't mutually exclusive.* You can go out and live your dreams and take risks and live a huge, daring, adventurous life, and still honor your responsibilities.

I knew as I sat there in my father's office that I could no longer expect or even desire his approval. All I could do was share my vision with him, knowing that it was mine to protect.

"So where are you going then?" he finally asked.

I breathed in deeply and began to tell him about watching *The Motorcycle Diaries.* I could see my father's face going gray, hearing about Che Guevara. Finally, he interrupted, "You're going to be a communist? I'm afraid you're a bit late for that, Leon."

"No," I half-heartedly countered, the confidence I had started with quickly splintering in front of the man I had been trying to impress my whole life. "I am going to travel across the world with no money."

"You're ridiculous," was my father's clipped reply.

And he was right. I was ridiculous. But big dreams demand that we engage with the ridiculous, that we possibly come off as crazy or unrealistic, that we might head straight for failure and unmitigated heartbreak. We might also be on the most adventurous road of our lives. We might be on the way to becoming our best selves.

At the time, I didn't have too many other details in place. All I knew was that I wanted to walk from one end of the world to the other, relying on the kindness of strangers.

The risks kept growing. Leave job. Leave home. Leave family. Leave country. Be accused of being ridiculous on a daily basis.

I could have given up right then in my father's office, wilting in front of his objections, but I didn't. I did the one thing I had feared doing my whole life: I lost my father's approval. And yet

Life is art.

there I was, still standing. In fact, I was more than just standing, I was quite possibly for the first time standing tall. I was no longer that awkward, bullied boy who strove for his father's approval. I was a man with a dream.

I stood over my father's desk as he remained seated in his chair. "It's what I am going to do. It's what I have to do."

Every choice we make comes with the risk of potential disasters and potential successes, and our lives are the masterpieces that we make of them. Each decision is a brushstroke on the canvas of who we are and who we wish to be. Some strokes will be precise and in one color, and others will splash in a passionate frenzy, messy and raw and more revealing than any carefully etched line.

I was about to risk it all for the chance at a life I could say I was proud of. No more half-life. No more living to the beat of another person's drum. I wanted to take charge of my canvas. I wanted to realize my own big dream.

We all have a big dream. Though not everyone will achieve their dream, success doesn't come in reaching it; success comes when we stand up and say we are willing to try. We are willing to take the risks, to break our hearts, to be called crazy and ridiculous and unrealistic. Because despite all the risks, you will find, as I have, the road that requires courage can be the path to joy.

What risks do we need to take in order to experience that joy? The Way of the Traveler isn't about booking the next flight; it is about dreaming the next big dream, whatever that might be for you.

What Is Your Big Dream?

We've all had lots of dreams over the years—different goals and plans, some more daring and ambitious than others. What is the one dream you're afraid to tell anyone about, because they are bound to look at you with disapproval and say, "You're being ridiculous?" What is the dream that's so audacious you've never spoken it anywhere other than in the private recesses of your soul? Big or small, crazy or sane, what is the one idea you never felt free to pursue?

Write down that big dream here.

_____

_____

_____

_____

_____

_____

_____

_____

_____

_____

_____

_____

_____

_____

_____

Now that you've written it down, you might want to start a journal to keep writing about it. Don't be afraid to add to it, to build upon it, to make it as crazy and elaborate and risky as you can imagine. Don't worry about failure and a broken heart—those come with the territory of being yourself.

Write as much as you want about what your dream means to you. And then set it aside . . . for now.

TRY IT DIFFERENTLY

Theodore Roosevelt said, "It is not the critic who counts; not the man who points out how the strong man stumbles. . . . The credit belongs to the man who is actually in the arena, whose face is marred by dust and sweat and blood . . . who at the best knows in the end the triumph of high achievement, and who at the worst, if he fails, at least fails while daring greatly."

Brené Brown discusses this concept in her book *Daring Greatly*, whose title came from Roosevelt's quote. As a researcher in social work and human behavior, Brown recognized that our vulnerability, our willingness to suffer indignities and to endure heartbreak, is in fact what empowers our ability to take risks, to dare greatly.

After I left my father's office, I went for a long walk. It was a gray and wet and cold afternoon. People hurried quickly past me on the streets of London. They were all heading home from work, stress etched into their faces. I couldn't imagine more years sitting in front of that slab of wood I called a desk. I was making money, but felt like I was making nothing of my life. I was twenty-seven and thought the time to make a change was now or never (though I have since realized that you can make a change at any age).

But as much as I wanted to take that big risk, to live that big dream, to strive valiantly, I also recognized that sometimes we have to alter our plans before we enter the arena.

Because the other thing about having a big dream is that it's really just a starting point. After sitting down with a map of the world, I became overwhelmed. How was I really going to cross the globe . . . with no money? My father was right, I decided. There was no way this was going to work.

Thankfully, I have a friend named Steve. We should all have a friend like Steve. Steve had gone to university to be a physicist. Now, I'm not quite sure what a physicist does every day, but after trying it out for a few years, Steve decided he wasn't too interested in what one does, either. In fact, he never had been. He had always done well in science, so his parents nudged him to attend a university that focused on physics and other incredibly smart-people stuff. But after graduating with his degree in physics, Steve decided to quit his profession before he even began. Because Steve didn't love science. He loved movies. Again the great debate: tomato v. orange.

"It was what I always wanted to do. I knew it, in that secret way you know things before you realize you do," he told me during our first meeting. "I just didn't know I could do it. I didn't know I could disappoint the people I loved and still be okay. It wasn't easy. Some days when there's no work, or a project doesn't get greenlit, it's still not. But it's what I had to do."

What is it going to take to give everything you have?

Steve and I had been introduced because one of my clients was interested in investing in a movie project Steve was working on. Long after the investor pulled out of the project, Steve and I remained friends. Perhaps even more than that, Steve became my role model. I saw how he was able to follow his dreams even when everyone else in his life had molded a different plan for him. Steve wasn't just a friend; he was who I hoped to be.

After I got home from that long walk, I decided that I needed to call someone who had done what I was attempting to do, someone who had shed the life chosen for him in favor of the one he was meant to live. So I called Steve. And Steve told me the three words I needed to hear: Try it differently.

He explained that in physics, there is a concept called the butterfly effect. Sometimes the smallest change in the initial condition of an action can lead to a very different outcome.

"Maybe you just need to change your initial conditions," he suggested. "In order to get the outcome you want."

I wanted to travel. I wanted to connect with strangers. I wanted to be out there in the world, raw and vulnerable and very determinably at risk. I wanted joy.

I decided that maybe the world was too big. Like a modern-day Goldilocks, I decided that America was just right. Plus, it was the land of opportunity. Manifest destiny. Pioneer spirit. All that jazz.

But then there was the issue of money. Steve was actually the one who suggested I take some.

Emotional stretching is critical; otherwise, we fail to grow.

"I mean, at least, you can use it to make a phone call or get on a bus, or something."

I decided on five dollars, though Steve thought I would have done better with twenty dollars.

"No," I explained. "Twenty dollars is enough to get me by. I don't want to get by. I want to connect."

So five dollars a day it was . . . in America. I would have

to find food, lodging, and transport along the whole journey from the people I met along the way. When I was a kid I was obsessed with the book *Robinson Crusoe*. Looking back, I can see it was really just a sales pitch for colonialism, but back then, to me, it was the story of an adventurer who got lost at sea, and lived shipwrecked for thirty years, encountering cannibals, captives, and mutineers. As a kid, I dreamed of a life at sea, where I, too, would encounter strange people and foreign lands. And now, I was planning to do just that. I would be shipwrecked in America, and I knew the only way I was going to survive was through the help of the people I met along the way. So I set "sail" to America, with a crazy idea and a restored faith in fearless wonder.

Not that I had any bloody clue what I was doing. All I knew was that I was going to run headlong into the adventure. I was going to throw out every rule about how it should be done, and instead, I was going to just do it (thank you very much, Nike). Far too often, we allow the perfect to become the enemy of the good. In our quest to make things happen exactly as we believe they should, we lose sight of the organic process of dreams. But when we learn to be flexible, to allow faith to be our flashlight and fate to be our companion, we are able to let go of the *how* and the *if* and instead, we embrace the Way of the Traveler.

What Are Your First Steps to Your Big Dream?

Pull your wild and crazy dream out again, the one you have written down on pages 27–28. Instead of letting yourself become overwhelmed, think of three things you could do today to start realizing your dream. Maybe you want to write and produce a play. Today, you could come up with a theme for it. Maybe you want to start your own shoe company. Today, you could sign up for a class on running a small business. Think of three actions that are absolutely realistic in working toward your big dream, and write them down here:

1. _____
_____
_____
_____
_____

2. _____
_____
_____
_____
_____

3. _____

_____

_____

_____

_____

The journey doesn't begin the moment you first step foot on the path, it begins when you first hear the call of the eagle, when you recognize that first sunrise of your new life, when you know, in your heart, that's its time to stop following the rules, and instead, start following your dreams. It can begin as simply as collecting photos of what that dream might look like, or finding a fellowship of people who share the same dream.

The Way of the Traveler can begin at any time. Does that mean that we always stay the course? No. There are times when I have experienced the joy and hope of the Way of the Traveler, as I did in Nepal, only to forget its call to adventure when I returned home to my job and life in London. But here's the real challenge, and the real promise: You can always return to the Way of the Traveler. It is available to you at any time; it is waiting for you right now.

THE ART OF THE HUSTLE

Six months later, I landed in Times Square. Sirens whirled around me. The hum of the crowds merged with the weight of my thoughts. Even the lights of the imposing billboards couldn't block out the reality of what I was about to do. I looked around and suddenly it was as though time stopped for a moment. The cars slowed, the voices quieted, and a soft voice floated through my heavy thoughts, "This is what you have always wanted, Leon. This is the life you were meant to lead."

As I reached out to random New Yorkers, however, asking them for help, I began to think this might be more the Way of the Guy Who Tried to Travel, but Then Had to Go Home and Drink Tomato Juice. Not one person in New York seemed to understand or want to help me in my terrifying, ridiculous, impossible dream.

Don't tell yourself "I can't."

I wandered the streets, crossing through the heavy traffic, making my way through the onslaught of tourists who didn't seem to care much about my big dream. I finally made it out of the Times Square bustle. I wasn't even sure where I was going, and as the crowds began to dissipate and the bright lights and over-bearing banners of Times Square faded into the gray and weary streets of a quieter New York, I began to wonder whether I had taken the right route. I saw a large anonymous building looming in the distance, a convoy of buses moving around it: the Port Authority Bus Terminal. Perfect, I thought, hoping someone would be kind enough to offer me a ticket west. Otherwise, I might begin to doubt my great, big, utterly ridiculous dream.

"Watch where you're going, man!"

I hadn't even realized I had bumped into someone, but apparently, my doubt had pushed my gaze to the ground and away from the world around me. Doubt has that effect. I was about to apologize and move on, but then I thought about what this stranger had just said to me: Watch where you're going!

That was exactly what I was trying to do. Instead of aimlessly moving through life, bumping into people and failing to create connection, I wanted to watch where I was going, and meet people heading in the same direction.

"Excuse me," I began. "I could apologize and move on, but I'm actually wondering if you can help—"

To my surprise, the man had stopped, along with his female companion. I soon learned that their names were Don and Dominica. They were street hustlers of the oldest sort, Dominica being a lady of the night, and Don being her, shall we say, agent. Don was lean and wiry, his frame moving so quickly it was hard to keep up with him. His mouth was just as quick.

"Man, ain't no wonder no one's helping you," he interrupted.

"What?" I began timidly.

"You ain't got no story."

Dominica nodded in agreement, as though my lack of story was clear to all of New York.

"See," Don began to explain, "everyone in New York, man, everyone in the world, they all got a story."

"You gotta tell ya story," Dominica echoed.

"Yeah," Don concurred. "Otherwise, no one will listen to you."

I didn't know how to say it then, and it took me a bit longer to realize, but sharing your story is about the scariest thing you can do. Was I really supposed to be telling Don and Dominica and every other person in Manhattan that I was a depressed and miserable person, that I didn't know what to do with my life, that going across America on five dollars a day was the best idea I had had in a long time?

After sharing as much with Don and Dominica, I asked, losing all faith in my own great dream, "You think anyone is going to want to help a desperate English chap who quit a good job to cross America with only five dollars in his pocket?"

"Yeah, man," Don slapped me on the back as we walked, outpacing me as we made our way down one of the long blocks around the bus station. "You got to tell them the tough stuff. That's how you hustle."

Don and Dominica told me that they were heading to New-ark. "I know it ain't no Hollywood sign, but we can get you to Jersey," Don offered.

It was the nicest thing anyone had said to me all day. As Don and Dominica and I made our way through the Port Authority, I began to realize that a risky, scary, in-the-middle-of-the-ring life demands that we share our story.

Not only do we have to figure out our puzzle pieces, but we also need to see how their arrangement is ultimately at the foundation of our big dream. What Don called a hustle, I call connection. It is through our vulnerabilities, through telling our authentic stories and experiences, those unique childhood histories and individual truths, that we take the biggest risk, but as a result, we get to connect with the world around us.

On the way to the train, Dominica bought me a hot dog and some fries. I could tell that she had little money herself as she slipped crumpled ones out of her purse to buy me the meal. I pulled out my $5, and tried to offer it.

"No." She smiled. "You might need that later."

As Dominica and I walked, she told me, "I think it's real special what you're trying to do. Most people won't get it, you know? But I think meeting new people, like how we're meeting, well, you know, it's nice to get to help people, too."

She smiled softly as Don bounded on ahead of us, shouting back, "I'm glad we found you."

Most of us innately understand the joy of receiving—even little children love getting gifts on Christmas morning or at birthday parties—but very few of us learn to similarly appreciate the joy of giving. Dominica did. So there I was, a former altar boy riding on the train with a pimp and a prostitute and the best hot dog I had ever eaten in my life.

As the train pulled into Newark, Don told me, "You know, lots of people got dreams. Not a lot of people get to see them get real. Don't give up, okay?"

So, don't give up, okay?

We can all see those dreams get real. We can grow up having tried tomato juice enough times to know it's not what we want. It's not what we've ever wanted, and we can begin not only to understand, but also to share the story of who we really are. And though our faces may get "marred by dust and sweat and blood," though we might fail, at least we will have done so by daring greatly.

Because here is the greatest reward you get from taking risks: faith. Faith that when we jump off the cliff, we will land in the water below. Faith that the Dons and Dominicas will show up just when we need them the most.

As my journey showed me (and I hope it is showing you a little, too), the Way of the Traveler is fueled by faith that everything is a part of an order we may not understand. It is so vast—spanning back into the ages of eternity and outward to the solar systems beyond—that our finite minds will never be able to understand the trajectory on which we all live. But it is there, silent and breathing and running just underneath the course of all of our lives. But if we don't jump, if we don't take risks, we never get the opportunity to see that faith will rise to greet us. Instead, we live in the darkness of believing it's not there. We look at the sorry world around us, and say, "Where is the miracle in this?"

When we set out to make our big dreams happen, we are connecting back into that magic of childhood, the hope and belief that anything is possible. We find again that fearless wonder that used to propel us through the backyards of friends as we were being pursued by dragons. We connect once again with the heroes and princesses and unicorns living within each of us. We stop walking around, looking at the ground, mired in doubt, and we begin to see for the first time the people of this world who are also willing to take a risk. Even if it costs them a train fare to Newark and a two-dollar hot dog.

As inspirational speaker and writer Iyanla Vanzant once shared on her Facebook page, "It's important that we share our experiences with other people. Your story will heal you and your story will heal someone else. When you tell your story, you free yourself and give other people permission to acknowledge their own story."

How Can You Share Your Story?

Now it's your turn. Who can you share your story with today? Who can you tell about the puzzle pieces that make you who you are? Write their names down and how you plan to reach out to them. Be honest with the world, and it will have no choice but to listen to you.

_____

_____

_____

_____

_____

_____

_____

_____

By stepping out of our everyday lives, we risk the wrath of everyone we know and love. Our parents might question us. Our partners might try to dissuade us. Our friends might cautiously ask, "Are you sure?"

But once you begin living those parts of your creative DNA, you'll know you're on the right path. You'll be able to look back at all those disparate pieces of the jumbled puzzle, and your purpose will slowly become illuminated.

Create space for something new to enter.

As I made my way across America, I knew I had made the right decision. I had been making the right decisions all along. Like the butterfly effect, once I made that initial decision, everything else fell into place. And the faith I was discovering told me that everything was happening just as it was supposed to be.

And then something else began to happen. I began to realize that my journey of self-discovery was becoming less and less about me. It was becoming about everyone I met on my journey, about those moments of kindness and adventure and even fear. At every turn, I was reminded that there are no rewards without taking risks. Danger reminds us what is sacred, and it doesn't just take us from the cliff to the water below. It allows us to hurdle through space, the wind whipping against our bodies, our hearts racing, knowing as fully as we are ever going to know that the reward is almost always worth the risk.

WHERE DO WE GO FROM HERE?

Nepal, *The Motorcycle Diaries*, Times Square: The adventure was on. Seeking the Way of the Traveler had become my life. But here's the thing: I still had no clue what I was doing. All I knew was that whatever I was doing, I was doing it fearlessly. Something I had never done before. And if I—awkward, bullied, misfit Leon—can do it, I have no doubt you can, too.

We all have the ability to envision that big dream. To do it differently. To do something dangerous.

It is time.

You know it.

I know it.

When I arrived at the Hollywood sign a month later, crossing the finish line barely mattered. Getting to California on $5 a day, though the initial plan, had become more of an afterthought in the end. The connections had become the destinations. Each relationship formed another constellation in the vastness of this universe, another piece of faith's evidence that I was doing the right thing, another light guiding me through unavoidable moments of doubt, rising up like scattered stars to remind me that my vulnerabilities and my fears were actually the building blocks of my own courage.

After my trip was completed, I was ready to start my new

life. The only problem was I had no idea what my new life was supposed to look like. Was I going to go back home? Absolutely not. Was I going to continue living off five dollars a day in Hollywood? Um, not likely. So guess what I did?

I got a desk job. In Los Angeles. I realized that in between my great adventures I also needed stability. So here we are, friends, at the end of our first adventure together, and I guess the question is, where do we go from here?

I know that quitting one's job and moving halfway around the world to travel across America on five dollars a day isn't for everyone, but we all have that crazy dream. As you will see, the Way of the Traveler isn't about getting stamps in a passport; it's about seeing your life as the greatest adventure of all. It's about recognizing that we all have the right and the ability to connect back to that childhood magic. To discover, once again, the fearless wonder of what life can hold once you begin embracing who you really are, and connecting with fellow travelers and accidental teachers along the way. If we think of risks as opportunities, they also become daring invitations to the lives we were meant to lead.

What if I told you that can happen right now?

Your life can change forever in this moment.

Because today is a great day to finally live!

TWO

THERE'S NO WAY TO DO THIS ALONE

"Alone we can do so little. Together we can do so much."

—HELEN KELLER

There are some moments you never forget. It was another day at school, which was never a good thing for me. I was fifteen and in my second year of high school.

I feared school every day. I woke up in the morning with a tight knot in my stomach, unsure of what humiliations I was bound to face that day. Some days were innocuous enough. I was able to hang about the schoolyard with the small group of friends who managed to fly just low enough under the radar that the bullies failed to notice them. On those days, they failed to notice me, too.

But some days, there was something about me that the bullies just couldn't resist. For a long time, I thought it was because I was a "loser" or a "pizza face" (one of their favorite insults once the acne appeared) or whatever cruel nickname they had conjured up for me that day. I thought it was because I, in my deepest heart and the sweetest recesses of my soul, invariably sucked. I thought it was me.

And to a certain extent, it was. As I grew older, I found that the word "loser" could easily be substituted for "sensitive." And that all the cruel nicknames meant that I *was* different from everyone else. I didn't think or act or feel like anyone else, and that was amazing.

Because as much as it was about me, it was also about them.

The bullies sensed that if I wasn't kept down, I might become stronger than they could ever be.

But that day, those schoolyard bullies were still in charge. And they had found new ways to make my life hell.

I was in a photography class at the time, and we had just completed a self-portrait project. I had taken a photo of myself but had accidentally left the picture in the darkroom the day before. Unfortunately, the bullies found it.

When I walked into school that day, I saw my face. Everywhere. The bullies had made copies of the photo and then added their own embellishments, putting me behind jail bars, drawing in more pimples than were in the original. They wrote those words again all over the copies—"loser," "pizza face," even "asshole." Every copy stabbed at my heart in new ways. And everywhere I turned, they reminded me that the bullies were in control and I was simply drifting along in their sea of cruelty.

I walked through school that morning, with that ever-present knot tightening inside me. My heart sank through my body, the color draining from my face, and the terrible abyss of feeling like I didn't have a friend in the world consumed me. It was hard enough being targeted by a group of boys who had somehow made it their life's mission to make my life miserable, but now I was the laughingstock of the whole school. I was learning very quickly that people were capable of being danger-ous and cruel. That it was better to be an island than to swim in the sea of humanity. I wasn't even sixteen, and yet I was profoundly shut down emotionally. As I walked through the halls of school that morning, the other kids' laughter echoing in my ears, I wondered whether life was really worth the pain.

And then I met a woman who changed my life, a guest speaker at school only a few months after my vandalized face had been wallpapered across the halls.

"My son died in the Middle East in 1992. And not for one day, do I regret the life he lived," were the first words out of her mouth.

The speaker's son was a photojournalist who had traveled all over the world taking pictures of different cultures and different countries, even when they were at war. The speaker continued, talking about how she had never really known her son until after he had died.

"My son and I became best friends after his death," she ex-plained. "Through the stories of his life, I found comfort, but more than that, I found inspiration. He didn't just live life for himself; he made the world better around him. His friends painted a picture of someone who always gave back. He was the person who played soccer with kids in the street. He was the friend you wanted by your side. He was the son I always wanted."

I looked around at all the kids who had laughed at me only a few months before, and suddenly, I didn't feel so angry. I actually felt compassion. Maybe we were all just trying to figure it out. Maybe we all had adventures lying before us, ones that would take us into the wilderness of our own hearts, and out into the world. And maybe, just maybe, I wouldn't have to do that alone.

I heard that speaker in a way I had never heard anyone before. There was something about her son's story that called to me, that offered just that little wisp of hope that I needed to believe that my life wasn't always going to look like this, that the world was bigger than the bullies that plagued me. Maybe, in fact, there was a world beyond my hometown of London, beyond my neighborhood, beyond school. And maybe, just maybe, I would be able to embrace the magical part of my childhood while escaping the sadness and depression that had haunted far too many other days of my early life.

That speaker was the first accidental teacher to enter my life, showing up just when I was ready. Our lives are filled with these teachers, who show us the truths we cannot see elsewhere in our lives.

I remember once hearing a story about an old man sitting at a bar. The old man declared loudly that he didn't believe in God.

"Why not?" the bartender asked.

"I was on my dogsled, crossing the frozen Yukon, when a terrible storm came up. I completely lost my way. The dogs and I huddled together for warmth but soon all our food was gone. Day after day, I begged God to help me but nothing, only silence. I knew I was going to die."

Surrender to your innate intelligence.

"But you're here," said the bartender. "God must have helped you."

"What God?" said the man. "Some Eskimo came and showed me the way."

Often, we mistake the great miracles in life as coincidences. We don't recognize the hand of fate even when it's knocking at our front door. But if we're willing to see that destiny is at work, then we will begin paying attention to the Eskimos who populate our world, offering us help, but even more than that, drawing us to our rightful path.

And those Eskimos do show up, often when we least expect them. They come to show us the way, even if we can't always see or understand that in the moment.

That speaker was one of my first Eskimos, one of my first accidental teachers. And though the seed she planted took a few more years to germinate, the story of her son's life forever changed my own.

ACCIDENTAL OPPORTUNITIES

When that seed decided to blossom, I had just graduated from university, and though that day in high school was only a few years behind me, it felt like a lifetime away. I had a group of friends who understood me. I was twenty-three years old and in my first year working as a broker. It was a year after I had gone to Nepal, and yet not much had changed in my life.

I was living in my first apartment, independent and on my own. I was on the early road of adulthood, and yet the memory of standing on that balcony in Kathmandu, knowing there was so much more to the world, haunted my daily life. So when the opportunity came up at work for someone to travel to Panama and take a banana boat across the Panama Canal, I couldn't help but remember the story of that woman's son, the photo-journalist who had embraced the wilderness of life.

I felt as though I were sitting back in that school auditorium, the speaker telling us, "My son would get on any boat, any plane. He would get in any car if he felt the adventure was going to introduce him to the world."

Accidental opportunities often show up when we least expect them. Sometimes we are aware of how powerful they are; sometimes we don't think much about them. Sometimes, we don't accept their challenge, failing to see the opportunity to be courageous that they present. The Way of the Traveler helps us to recognize those accidental opportunities. It asks us to say "yes" even when we're not exactly sure why.

And there it was, on a Wednesday morning in the conference room I was quickly learning to abhor, that my boss presented me with the first major accidental opportunity of my life. I would take the banana boat through the Panama Canal, and I would come back and report on its potential for financial investment.

What I didn't expect was that it would also reintroduce me to my mum.

What Are Your Accidental Opportunities?

Take a look at your own life history and identify three accidental opportunities—perhaps a temporary job that turned into the career of a lifetime, or the time you found a stray dog that became your best friend.

1. _____

_____

_____

_____

2. _____

_____

_____

_____

3. _____

_____

_____

_____

_____

As you look over these opportunities, also reflect on any you have missed. When did you say "no" when you should have said "yes"? Are there any accidental opportunities that you are ignoring in your life today?

ACCIDENTAL HEROES

Two weeks later, I flew to Colón, the city on the north end of the Panama Canal. It was my first time in Central America, and I was ready to be introduced to the world. I studied plenty of things at university, but I was an expert in nothing. To a certain extent, that hasn't changed much since. What I have learned from my journeys is that I can't truly experience a place if I am not willing to learn from it. The Way of the Traveler bars us from being experts. Once we are experts, we shut down, we lose our curiosity, we think we know too much.

The Way of the Traveler demands that we stay students, learning from the chorus of teachers that surrounds us if we're only willing to listen. But I've got to admit, listening is one of the hardest things to do. That's why sometimes the world has to shake us up in order for us to pay attention. As I walked the streets of Colón, I had little idea how much I was about to be shaken.

I left my hotel and decided to stop at a grocery store. I know, I know, real adventurous, Leon. But on my quick trip to pick up some bottled water, I noticed a security guard standing in the corner of the store, carrying a fully automatic weapon. That should have been a sign to go back to my hotel, but I decided, no, I was going to be introduced to the world. I asked the guard what the gun was for, and he said, while barely looking at me, "The bad ones."

Align yourself with the flow.

I continued on through the city, marveling at the old churches, the buildings that reminded me of an overgrown French Quarter, with vines weaving through their architecture. I breathed in the sea air, and remembered again the speaker's words, "Any boat, any plane . . ." I had done it. I had taken the accidental opportunity, I was being introduced to the world. I felt free, released from the life I had been living and into the one I was always meant to live.

And then I was introduced to another part of the world: its underbelly. A small group of men suddenly surrounded me. I felt whisked back to my days of being bullied, the same fear and adrenaline engulfing my system.

One of the men demanded, in broken English, "Your money!"

My money, I thought. I had the equivalent of about $50

on me, which I was happy to part with if that meant saving my life. But fear took over, paralyzing my hand as I attempted to reach for the cash, slowing down every moment and movement until I could barely move at all.

Next thing I knew, there was a very strong fist jabbing me in the stomach. I was outnumbered. Four to one. I should have paid more attention during karate. I tried to get to the money, but they were quicker than I was, emptying my pockets of my cell phone and my fifty dollars. I was about to breathe a sigh of relief, hoping the attack was over when another fist came at me, hitting me across the face and knocking me to the ground. I cried out, not knowing what else to do, as the men began to kick me, their heavy boots and shoes jamming into my ribs and shoulders, their own fear mutating into brutal kicks to my stomach. All those years of worrying about my future and whether life would ever get "better" were expunged with each blow. I didn't care about what people thought of me, or whether I was living the right life; I just wanted to live.

I felt a few more blows and then all of a sudden it ended. Like a quick afternoon thunderstorm that disappears as quickly as it arrives, my perpetrators had taken off, and in their place stood the security guard from the grocery store, his unnecessarily large weapon in hand.

He nodded in the thieves' direction, "The bad ones."

I was so shaken I didn't know what to do. To this day, I am not sure I even thanked him. He didn't know me, and yet he had been willing to step in to save me. Him and his assault rifle, but I imagined if a grocery store security guard had access to such weapons, so did the "bad ones."

"No good to be alone, my friend. Bad things happen this way," he warned.

He walked off just as it hit me (much like those punches to the gut), that this stranger had just possibly saved my life. And his words joined the speaker's, echoing in my ears, "No good to be alone."

That security guard became an accidental hero that day. In Robert Putnam's book *Bowling Alone*, he talks about how our world has become devoid of social capital, our ability to create invisible social networks through which communities connect. Science has shown that these invisible networks govern the bulk of human interaction. We are hardwired to sense when someone is a threat; but we are also hardwired to sense when someone is offering empathy, when someone is being kind. These invisible connections create a network that wraps around the world, embracing us all if we're willing to connect into it. But if we are surrounded by people who threaten us, who don't foster empathy and kindness, we retreat as though from a physical threat. We become isolated and alone, trapped in front of a computer or TV screen, unable to create any relationships with the world around us.

Pay attention to the world.

The world I grew up in seemed to be socially impoverished.

Kids stood by while I was mercilessly teased. Teachers failed to stand up for me, even when I was being beaten up. But as I journeyed out into the world, I found out there are so many cultures rich in these networks. People protecting one another, connecting with one another, not out of fear, but out of trust. That day, the security guard didn't show up because he felt like playing the hero. He showed up because that's what he would have done on any day. He was an accidental hero because he was just being human.

Who Are Your Accidental Heroes?

Who have been the accidental heroes in your life? At some point or another, there have been people who have saved us, who said the right words, or did the right deeds, to steer us onto the proper course. Being a hero doesn't mean we have to save someone's life; it just means showing up at the right time to offer someone a different path. We have all had those people. The ones that sometimes gently, sometimes with greater force, have pulled us out of the muck, and reminded us that we are not alone. Write down three of them here:

1. _____

_____

_____

2. _____

_____

_____

3. _____

_____

_____

Now, think about a time when *you* were that person. As you move through your day, see where there are opportunities to be one again. Is it helping someone move a box at the office? Is it waiting with an elderly person who has locked themselves out of their house? In order to be an accidental hero, we have to be willing to pay attention to the world around us. Where does it need our help? That invisible energy between people doesn't always have to happen in moments of crisis. It can also come when we take the opportunity to honor someone else's struggles, to help them carry, however temporarily, the heavy load of life, and for a brief, flickering moment, be reminded just how precious that life is.

ACCIDENTAL SHIPMATES

They say it takes a village to raise a child, but actually, it takes a village to raise an adult, too. Sadly, in today's world, too many of us believe that we don't need other people. We think there is a special prize for doing it alone. We take pride in our solo performances, and we forget the beauty of the symphony. But if we want to grow, if we want to look out onto the world and feel its embrace, we need to be willing to join it. And once we are willing, the world will quickly rush to join us.

I have experienced this time and time again. Some have come to my rescue, but more often, they have given me direction, shifting my energy—taking me out of that darkness of fear or desperation, and leading me into the light of hope.

Which brings us to our accidental shipmates, the village that rises up around us if we're willing to let them. For so much of my life, I refused to let anyone in. I feared they would turn into those bullies who haunted my childhood. I didn't want to be hurt like I had by them, and yet I couldn't help myself from wanting to reach out. I wanted friends. I wanted to fall in love. I wanted to be a part of the world.

As I began to grow (and I mean that literally, as I got taller and less awkward) and finally changed schools and got away from the bullies, I began to meet those shipmates—fellow passengers on this ship of life whose mere presence offers us the peaceful knowledge that it's okay to be who we are.

The next morning, after my encounter in the dark alley, I walked onto the banana boat with bruised ribs and a swollen cheek. The sailors all expected a businessman to board their ship. I am sure they didn't know what to do with an exhausted guy in cargo shorts who looked like he had been trying out for *Rocky XV*. Vassili was the captain, and the first person to approach me.

"You okay, Mr. Logothetis?" His concern seemed real, despite his stern demeanor.

I explained to him what had happened the night before, telling him about the security guard and his fateful warning.

"Smart man," Vassili agreed. "We all learn on the ship that you try to save yourself, you sink the whole ship. You try to save your shipmates, you live, too."

He walked off, leaving me to wonder whether the ship was sinking. Throughout the course of the day, I went over the numbers and figures with the captain, how much fuel the boat used, how quickly it could travel, how many bananas it could haul.

Vassili kept offering me the savory fare from the galley, but at the time, I had done my best to stay away from local foods in foreign lands. Sure, I would try the tourist-approved restaurants, but the fish soup on a banana boat in the Panama Canal?

"No, thank you," I tried to politely refuse. "Do you have some rice?"

Vassili consented to my request for rice, but I could tell he was bothered.

For those who don't know, the Panama Canal is a fifty-mile, man-made waterway that links the Atlantic to the Pacific Ocean. Our ship was heading to Ecuador on the Pacific side, and after a day making our way through the narrow channel, we found ourselves released into the Pacific Ocean.

As I stood on the deck, one of the other sailors came out to watch as we made our way into the Pacific.

"Yes, it is very beautiful."

"Oh, it is," I replied, somewhat surprised that one of the sailors was talking to me. I was again on the outside of the circle. I was a foreigner. I was there on business. It was clear that I didn't fit with these grizzled men of the sea, even with my swollen cheek.

Contraction and expansion are the dance of life.

"The captain, he said you get beat up," the sailor continued.

I was expecting to be ridiculed. I knew what happened when you were on the outside of a group. You are the fool.

"It was no big deal," I began.

"I am doctor," the sailor informed me. "I can make sure . . ." He searched for his words. "You are not too bad hurt."

But I was still caught on "doctor." "How are you a doctor? What are you doing here?"

He looked out back to the Pacific and smiled, "I love the sea."

As I found out, Fedir had been a doctor in the Ukraine until the economy pushed him out of work. He ended up finding a job on an international ship as a doctor, at which point he fell in love with the ocean. When that job ended, he learned how to work a ship, and gave up his medical career for one that guaranteed him a place on the open seas.

Fedir took me inside and determined that my bruised ribs were only that.

"It would have not been safe to have broken rib at sea," he explained.

"Why not?" I asked, having never been "at sea" nor had a broken rib.

"Soon, we will be in ocean. Far away in ocean. Not safe."

Later, when it was time for dinner, Fedir invited me to sit with his friends and fellow shipmates. The banana boat, as everyone there called it, was actually a large refrigerated reefer that transported bananas by the tons. We had picked up the boat in Panama, and were heading to Ecuador where the crew would load the bananas, ultimately transporting them across the Atlantic Ocean to Europe. The boat held a crew of twenty-five to thirty men, all from Russia and the Ukraine. On that ship, I planned to cross the ocean and meet the world.

When large bowls of meaty stew were passed around, I looked for some bread, wondering if I could ask for rice. Vassili's heavy hand fell on my shoulder.

"Eat," he commanded. The other men looked at me. Peer pressure. And not the good kind. My hand once again refused to move, as I looked into the meaty porridge in front of me and began to feel seasick.

"We have long travels in front of us, friend," Vassili offered. My shipmates nodded in agreement. "You will want to be well nourished."

Fedir added, as he slurped the first spoonful, "It's good."

What could I do? It was either risk mad cow disease or risk banishment from the crew.

"Do you have a ham sandwich?" was my cowardly reply.

I could see the captain and Fedir were disappointed, maybe even a bit insulted, as Vassili went to tell the galley to prepare a ham sandwich. I tried my best to rejoin the merriment of the table, even as my gaffe nagged at me.

There are so many times in life when we pull ourselves out of a group just as quickly as we entreat our way in, and quickly, we feel the energy shift. Those friendly bonds suddenly dissipate like the waves in the ocean. And in their dissipation, we are often left with the admonishments of our own mind, separating us even further from others.

After dinner, we took turns swimming in the pool. And by pool, I do not mean the crystalline waters of a Carnival cruise ship. The banana boat pool was more like a small hole on the deck filled with some questionable water, but I jumped in. I wanted to join my accidental shipmates in not just the work, but also the fun. For too much of my life, I had sacrificed fun because of fear. I had become so good at following the rules that I failed to have any fun. Sometimes the only way to connect with others is to break the rules. We must jump in. We must find a way to leave behind inner admonishments in order to join the camaraderie of the group. As I sat in the tub, laughing with my fellow shipmates, I felt a part of the world.

As I went to bed, I thought about all the things I had learned in just two short days: that it was no good to be alone, and that when in doubt, jump in.

As Conrad wrote in *Heart of Darkness*, "Watching a coast as it slips by the ship is like thinking about an enigma . . . always mute with an air of whispering, 'Come and find out.'" I was finding out. I was discovering myself in a way that I never would in my London office. I wasn't sure yet what any of it meant. Sometimes I still don't. The Way of the Traveler doesn't always provide the answer. But it always offers the whisper, "Come and find out."

Expand your emotional bandwidth.

I woke up drenched in sweat. I wasn't sure what time it was, but I could tell it was the middle of the night. Something was wrong with my stomach . . . and it clearly wasn't heartburn.

No, it was more along the lines of that scene in *Alien*, when the alien emerges from that guy's intestines. The ship rolled along choppy waters, making the pain even more intense.

Was it the ham sandwich? Had I not only made myself feel alienated, but was I also sick now because of it? Too many times in life, we find ourselves back on the outside just when we thought we were in. It feels like we take two steps back for every step forward, and just when we think our ship has finally sailed, we wake up in the middle of the night, lying confused and sweaty in the dark, wondering what sort of mistake we just made.

I thought about calling for help, but then the crew would know I couldn't run with the big boys. I would be voted off the island just as quickly as I had been voted on. But as the morning sun rose above the waves, my pain became unbearable. It was time to call in the cavalry.

All of the traveling I have done since that banana boat trip has shown me that the only thing more dangerous than a poisonous ham sandwich is the poison in our minds. The Way of the Traveler clears that poison. It demands we take action, that we call for help even when our pride is busy telling us to stay in bed and ride it out alone.

I decided that Fedir and I had become close enough that perhaps he wouldn't tell anyone, so I sheepishly knocked on his door. He was just heading out to his shift, but saw my face and brought me into his room. He felt around my stomach, but when he applied pressure to my abdomen, I howled. It was like being punched by twenty fists in a Panama alley.

"Hmmm," Fedir replied, as I began to question his medical skills.

"It could be indigestion," he offered.

"It doesn't feel like indigestion," was my weary reply.

"Or it could be your appendix."

My appendix? Who gets appendicitis on a banana boat in the Pacific Ocean?

"I'll call the captain," Fedir began to head to the door.

"No," I stopped him, still not wanting to cause a scene. Maybe it was indigestion. What were they going to do, pull into the next port? All I could think was, "I should have eaten the beef stew."

"I'll take some more Tums," I offered. "Let's see how I feel by lunch."

By lunch, I could barely get out of bed. Thankfully, Fedir came in to check on me. He took one look and shook his head. "This bad, Leon."

I could barely speak from the pain. "I know," I replied.

That was the last thing I remember, before seeing the captain in front of me.

"Leon," he said, as I fought to focus through the pain. "We think there is something very wrong with you."

I nodded, feeling the sweat pour from my head across my face.

"We're going to bring you back to port," he explained. His words drifted in and out of my consciousness. "But it might take some time."

I was scared. This wasn't walking-into-school-and-seeing-my-face-photocopied-throughout-the-hallways scared. This was, oh-my-God-I-might-die scared. And suddenly my life, in all its twists and turns and accidental moments, became miraculously precious.

Thankfully, Fedir was there, along with an assortment of sailors, who kept me in a cold bath as the banana boat headed as swiftly as it could to the nearest port. I can remember various faces hovering over me during the next twelve hours, feeding me soup broth, pouring water in my mouth, pulling me in and out of the tub, and dressing me before laying me back in bed. Fedir stayed near, as the captain came in to let me know how close we were to port. The hours passed very slowly and very painfully. But there was never any doubt in my mind that I had become an accidental shipmate. My comrades cared for me as though I was one of their own, because I *had* become one of their own.

Who is your tribe?

They rallied together in a way I had rarely seen in my own life. I had not only been introduced to the world, I had been saved by it.

Who Are Your Accidental Shipmates?

We are never alone. On this ship of life, we all have those friends, family, and fellow adventurers, those faces that we would gladly bring with us on a desert island— because they all serve a role. One may be the doctor, while some make us laugh, some guide us, and some cool our fevered foreheads in the middle of the night. But they all teach us—not only how to live at sea, but also how to enjoy life on land. Who are your shipmates? Choose five of them, and write what each brings into your life. Just one or two words will do—humor, trust, love, thoughtfulness, danger.

1. _____

_____

2. _____

_____

3. _____

_____

4. _____

_____

5. _____

_____

And is there someone on your ship whom you don't really need? Because like the captain said, "You try to save yourself, you sink the whole ship." Who would only work to save him or herself? Maybe they're better off not on your ship. Maybe you're better off without them, too. Think about how you might be able to kindly distance yourself from their shores.

Since it takes a village to raise an adult, we need to be thoughtful when we decide who gets to live in the village. For too long, I had allowed people in who only beat me up. I was so focused on the bullies in my life that I failed to see my accidental shipmates—the friends who didn't think I was a loser. The friends who played with me in that schoolyard, and,

Align yourself with dreamers.

even from time to time, stood up for me when I was unable to stand up for myself. Friends like Fedir, who burst into my room just as we came into port at Puerto Bolívar in Ecuador, announcing, "Your mother is on her way!"

ACCIDENTAL REUNIONS

When I arrived in Puerto Bolívar, I was surprised to find that my mother had already made her way to Guayaquil, where the closest modern hospital was. At this point, I was barely able to breathe from pain, but there I was, in a two-seater plane that felt like it hadn't been serviced since 1977, heading to meet my mother as I flew across Ecuador. What the hell was happening?

When I arrived at the hospital, they quickly took X-rays to confirm what everyone had assumed was true. I had appendicitis, and during the hours it had taken for me to get to the hospital, my appendix had come close to rupturing.

The doctor walked into the room where my mother and I waited and announced, "You are lucky to be alive."

My mother shot me a look. When she had first heard about the trip, she had expressed her concerns. I had inherited my squeamishness about exotic foods and locales from her, after all. My mother believed that children were better off playing inside where it was warm. She feared pneumonia and floods and random acts of violence. She loved us so much she never wanted to see us get hurt, but what we fear the most often meets us halfway. Because by the time she clutched the bar of my hospital gurney as they rushed me down the hall, the doctors shouting in Spanish over both of our heads, I had already been hurt a lot. All I had left was the hope that this time, I wouldn't die.

On this five-day business trip to Panama, I was confronted with the terrible fragility of life, reminding me again of *Heart of Darkness*: "Like a running blaze on a plain, like a flash of lightning in the clouds. We live in the flicker."

I was living in the flicker. In fact, if one is to truly embrace everything the world has to offer, it's the only place to live. And as I looked over to my mother, who was holding my hand, I knew I wasn't alone. In fact, our relationships are what sustain the light; they keep the wick burning even on our darkest days.

The doctor told me in his broken English that I had to go to surgery immediately, as my appendix was about to burst. I signed a set of documents that were in Spanish. I don't speak Spanish. But it didn't matter. I was taken straight to the emergency room. The gas was administered, and then darkness ensued.

When I woke up in the recovery room, I was grateful not to be dead. At least I thought I wasn't dead. But what was my mother doing here? Though she had traveled with me, in my feverish haze, I had nearly forgotten that she was even in Ecuador. The trip to Guayaquil seemed like one long surreal dream.

Over the next few days, my mother and I did something we had never done before: We got to know each other. She told me about her childhood in Greece; I told her about my recent breakup with yet another girlfriend. And throughout that incredible accidental reunion, my mum and I became friends. I thought back to that speaker in high school, how she had become best friends with her son after he died. I remembered how I had thought to myself, "I need to spend more time with my mum." And how I had failed to follow through with that plan.

The irony wasn't lost on me that nearly dying had led to this opportunity, in a small hospital in the middle of Ecuador, with my mother sleeping in a cot beside my bed. That's the other thing about our "village." There are some people we invite into it, but we also need to remember the ones who lived there before us. The family who brought us into the world—our parents and grandparents, our aunts and uncles, who laid the bricks, however haphazardly, of our foundations.

Commit to those you love.

Often we forget those shipmates, the ones who show up for us so consistently that we presume they will always be there. We take them for granted; only realizing their importance when we need them most.

Who Should You Reunite with Today?

Who in your life deserves an accidental reunion? Because here's the other secret about accidents: Sometimes we can be the ones to cause them. We can choose to get on the ship or we can choose to stay on shore. And we can choose to reach out and make life happen.

So who do you need to reach out to today? Which elder do you know the least? Which person should you know the most? Write down two people with whom you should connect, and how you can make that connection happen. Will you take them to lunch, go on a trip? How will you get to know them before it's too late?

1. _____

_____

_____

_____

_____

_____

_____

2. _____

_____

_____

_____

_____

_____

_____

On my last day in Ecuador, as my mum and I prepared to head back to London together, I could tell she was beginning to worry about something else.

"Leon," she asked me. "You keep talking about how you want to live an adventurous life. . . ."

"Yeah," I replied, worried about the admonition that was sure to follow.

"Maybe that's what you need to do," and I could almost see the memories reflected in her eyes, memories of her wiping away my tears after yet another painful day at school. "Maybe that's what you always needed to do."

Adventure is in all of us. And it doesn't require a banana boat through the Panama Canal to discover it. It just requires that we be willing to see the guides around us, the people who can teach us, who can save us, who can connect us back to where we came from, even as we are trying to figure out where, exactly, we want to go.

When I made it home, I didn't have a single regret. Because my odyssey through the Panama Canal had introduced me to the world. From the crew on the banana boat to the doctor who saved me, they were all a part of my family. Sometimes we have to be far away from the people we love to realize the depth of that caring. And sometimes strangers come into our lives and reignite our love for the world. But without either of them, we remain alone, unprotected, afraid. We cannot go in search of the big dream alone. We need our tribe, we need our village, we need the "Me. We." of friendship to help us see those big dreams become real. If we aren't able to embrace those relationships, we will only find ourselves stranded on-shore, watching the great opportunities of life continue to pass us by.

THREE

THE WAY OUT OF THE COMFORT ZONE

"Your comfort zone is not a place that you want to remain in. Dare, discover, be all that you can be."

—CATHERINE PULSIFER

If you've learned anything by now, I hope you've learned this: I'm no expert. In anything, really. Jack-of-all-trades, master of none. But the one thing I am pretty sure of is this: Life can be a really uncomfortable place, and sometimes that's the best place to be.

The way I look at it, comfort zones are like hot tubs. Sure, when you step into one, it feels great—warm water, the sound of a whirling tub, a jet stream of bubbles shooting against your back—but have you ever spent three days in one? Precisely. Because that warmth, that comfort, those soothing jets would have you cooked and pruned in twelve hours. That's what a comfort zone does, too. It feels great at first. Your immediate stresses seem to melt away; the comfort of routine takes over; but then we realize (often far too late), that we have become pruned.

It's not necessarily our fault. It is part of human nature to seek comfort. In the midst of paying bills and buying groceries, finding a job or trying to keep one, taking the time and effort to live our dreams just sounds like one more exhausting proposition on an endless to-do list. Instead, we just want to get through traffic, and come home to an easy dinner and a night on the couch. Who has the energy for self-discovery? But the problem is that what we think is comfort, what we call relaxation, is actually the one thing that separates us from real joy, because . . .

THE COMFORT ZONE IS A LIE

I am no stranger to comfort zones. I normally prefer to call them existential crises, but I'd say every few years, I find myself stuck in a grind that I thought I knew better than to get into. Routine grows over my passion like a deadly mold, and suddenly I won't remember why I cared about my work, or even my relationships, in the first place. Everything becomes stale, including—and especially—*me.*

Sadly, most people on this planet don't have the luxury of a comfort zone. They wake up hungry. They struggle to make ends meet. But though they would gladly trade places with those who buy warm beds in big-box stores, and keep a refrigerator full of food at all times, they also exhibit something that seems so hard to come by in our comfortable world: joy.

Because here is the biggest lie about the comfort zone—it does not make you happy. Growth takes place in discomfort. Progress is born out of problems. And joy is the natural counterpart to pain. Joy is not born from the isolation of a hot tub. It is built when people are forced to connect, whether out of shared

Give your fears to the winds.

desperation or shared passion. Far more people die from stress or loneliness or boredom than they do from scaling Mt. Kilimanjaro. But I never would have learned that on my own. I had to be willing to meet my next accidental teacher.

ESCAPING THE LIE

They say that when a student is ready, a teacher will appear, but in my case, it was when the student was desperate enough that he was willing to listen to the teacher. I had just turned thirty. I had gone across America and landed in Los Angeles. I had decided I was going to become a TV guy instead of a finance guy. And I was once again miserable. I found myself at a party, one of those affairs you really don't want to go to, but you think you should because of work, people, and connections. The only problem was, I couldn't leave the party. Because I was the fool hosting it.

I looked around. More than thirty people filled my living room, some of whom were good friends, others I had never met. Together, they sat around with wine glasses and appetizers, laughing and talking, and apparently having a good time. I was just waiting until the last person walked out the door so I could go back to bed and watch TV. Eventually, people did start to leave, as I patiently cleaned up around them, hoping they would get the hint. Then, as the last cluster of people began to edge their way toward my front door, I met him: Naasih.

I had seen Naasih throughout the night. He was either laughing or making people laugh. He seemed to command the room. In fact, had I not known whose house it was, I probably would have assumed he was hosting the party, which meant I wasn't really an immediate fan of Naasih.

As he was leaving, Naasih invited me to an upcoming storytelling event, where he was going to speak about his travels.

I said sure, knowing I would never go see this charismatic, likable fellow who had just taken over my party. But then Naasih took my number, and said he would call me to remind me. And then he called.

I agreed to meet him at the storytelling event the next night, taking place at a small nightclub on the west side of Los Angeles. I don't know why I said yes; maybe I had simply run out of excuses. Or maybe that window of opportunity had opened just enough for my own willingness to feel its breeze. Maybe I was just interested in hearing what someone else had to say about *their* life. It was as though I had no choice but to say yes. That night, I showered, got dressed, and left the house (a big deal for me that week), completely unaware that everything was about to change. Sometimes in order to escape our comfort zones, all we have to do is leave the house.

The irony is that for someone who had become housebound and depressed, I had always been a fan of escaping. Unfortunately, many of us escape through things that aren't good for us—through food or television or even alcohol and drugs. We escape through relationships and our job. We escape only to eventually find ourselves back in the prison we thought we were escaping. For me, I had started to escape through isolation, trading in one slab of wood in London for another slab of wood in LA. I had forgotten how to reach out for adventure. Naasih, in more ways than I could ever count, helped me to remember.

Drop into your heart from your mind.

What Are Your Great Escapes?

Now it's your turn. Take a look at your life. How do you escape today? What are five ways that you create "comfort"? For me, I'll go to see a movie in the middle of the day—when I should be at work. Or I'll hide in bed with a gallon of ice cream, knowing that both are only temporary salves. Some of your own escapes may indeed bring you real joy, but go ahead and circle the ones that you're not so sure of.

1. _____

_____

_____

_____

_____

2. _____

_____

_____

_____

_____

3. _____

_____

_____

_____

_____

4. _____

_____

_____

_____

_____

5. _____

_____

_____

_____

_____

I sat in the back of the club as Naasih captured the crowd with his charm, sharing his experiences of traveling by bus through Myanmar. He had witnessed some of the world's most heart-wrenching poverty, and yet he had created relationships unlike any that he had experienced on Grey-hound. He had shared food with a family of four who offered him what little stale bread they had. He had

Everything is energy.

slept on a withered seat with two men searching for work. He had tried his best to communicate in broken English, but eventually realized that words had very little meaning in comparison to the gestures he was sharing with others. Coming from a country with everything, he found himself in a country with nothing. And everything he thought he knew about life flew out the window of a rickety bus.

After the performances, I asked Naasih if he had time for some coffee. He graciously said good-bye to his friends and fans, and we headed out into the Los Angeles night.

Naasih mentioned that a mutual friend had told him about my adventures before the party—leaving my home, leaving my job, traveling across America on five dollars a day. "I thought I had surely found a kindred spirit," he said. "But then when I met you," he continued, "you weren't at all who I thought you would be."

"Why is that?" I asked, truly wanting to know what this man's impression of me was.

"It didn't seem like you were living what you learned," he said with a smile contrasting the words that he was about to say. "You seemed like an asshole."

My first reactions were anger, defensiveness, and a hearty dose of, "How dare he?" But then I thought about it. By retreating into my depression, I had once again started locking people out of my life. Instead of sharing my vulnerability, I was pretending that nothing and no one could touch me. I had become a lonely man who thought that throwing a party might prove I wasn't so lonely after all.

Because here is the thing I was just beginning to learn about the Way of the Traveler: Sometimes we take two steps forward only to take one step back. We gain insight and revelation, and then we forget them. But the beauty of the adventurous road is that the lesson is always there to be learned again.

I began to laugh, really laugh. Just like pain, the truth will set us free. It broke through the lie of my routine, and it showed me that my comfort zone of depression and self-pity had turned me into an asshole.

Naasih told me how he ran a program where he took people

through India. But it wasn't your usual travel-guide affair: "You won't have an agenda or even know what we're doing the next day. You won't have anything. All you will have is me."

"Well, that's certainly bold of you," I quipped.

He shot me a slight glare, one I would come to know quite well, before continuing warmly. "I will show you India like you have never experienced it," he promised. "There will be days where you will hate me for it. And there will be days where you will know that it was the only way for you to finally find what you're clearly not finding now."

"How long is the trip?" I asked him.

"One month."

Most of you are probably thinking that it would have been a good time, Leon, to run out of that coffee shop and never look back, but I knew he was offering me a chance to really escape. To take a courageous leap into a foreign adventure, to become transformed by an unknown world, and to return a more enlightened, joyful being.

Well, at least, that's what I hoped. I put down my grande latte, and said, "Let's do it."

CREATE A SENSE OF UNBALANCE

There is nothing that can prepare you for India. I have been to more than ninety countries, and to India several times, and even now, whenever I return, India doesn't greet me with a quiet handshake. It shakes me to my core the minute my foot hits land.

After two stops and too many hours, we landed in Delhi. I expected we would go to the nearest hotel and I would get the chance to take a nap and freshen up. How wrong could one man be? Freshening up was not on the agenda. Taking a nap was not on the agenda. What was on the agenda was an early-morning trip to a slum.

Naasih and I arrived in the slum just as the sun was breaking across the smoggy Delhi sky. It seemed as if those shanties stretched for miles, like an ocean of tin roofs and laundry lines of drying clothes. It was overwhelming to think of how many people lived in this majestic squalor, all determined to survive another day of poverty's cruel consequences. People were already emerging from the clapboard shacks they called home, and though sheets of metal and long fabric worked to mimic doors, we could still see inside, where many slept fitfully on the floor. Naasih led me down so many passageways and byways that I was sure we would never find our way back out. I hadn't slept in thirty hours; I hadn't eaten anything since the plane, and I was beginning to wonder whether the brightly colored shacks we were passing were actually just part of a strange dream I was having while sleeping soundly in my bed back home.

Finally, Naasih stopped and turned to me, "Give me your bag."

Okay, so maybe I was in a nightmare.

"Excuse me?" I asked, unsure of whether I had heard him correctly.

He gestured to the small knapsack I had been allowed to bring on the trip, repeating, "Your bag."

I handed it to him warily.

"And your shoes and socks," he added.

I had agreed to go along with this man. I had promised to follow his directions, and in return, I was hoping to find whatever I thought was missing from my life.

I reached down, took off my shoes and socks and handed them to him.

"And now your shirt," he commanded.

Though I could already feel the sun gaining strength, the early morning dawn held a chill. I shivered as I pulled off my shirt, leaving myself in only the jeans I had worn on the plane. I waited for him to ask for those, too, but evidently leaving me barefoot and shirtless was enough.

Naasih looked around, and said, "I'll meet you back here at sunset."

"Where?"

"Right here. Just ask someone where Rata Road is. They'll lead you back here."

"Where are you going?" I asked as he began to walk away.

He laughed, "Oh, I'm heading back to the hotel. Time for a nap."

Thanks, buddy, I thought, as it began to sink in that I had just been left in the middle of an Indian slum on the outskirts of Delhi with no shoes or even a shirt. And all the result of having agreed to go hear someone tell their story in a grimy club in Los Angeles.

I looked around at the shanties that surrounded me, the small and unstable structures that millions called home. I could see a cadre of rats running in the distance, ending their night of scavenging. The ground was hard-packed by rain and sun, creating a smooth path that snaked its way through the small shacks and the seemingly unending refuse that seemed to surround them. That was all I could see at first: the piles of stacked paper and plastic and cans and waste, and then there was the scent that was now just beginning to creep into my nose. It was the smell of burnt rubber, heavy and noxious in the smoggy air. I suddenly wanted to be sick, and I realized that if I didn't get some food soon, I probably would be.

I began to walk through the streets, hoping to run into someone who might be willing to help me. Oddly enough, no one paid too much attention to the tall, bald lunatic walking through their midst. Morning slowly began to shift into day as the sun beat down on me. My throat was dry, my stomach growling with hunger. It felt like the world was becoming a tilt-a-whirl, my head spinning from the heat and the people and the sheer terrifying exhaustion of landing in India and finding myself in the middle of one of

Are you willing to be yourself?

the most impoverished places on earth with no one to help me.

And then I saw it. It was a small shanty, but someone was clearly inside. Instead of a door, it had a large blanket covering the opening that read: "LA Lakers."

Seemed about as good a sign as any. I walked up to the shanty, and rapped softly on the tin that comprised its walls.

A young, skinny man, no older than twenty-five, came to the "door." You could say he looked more than mildly surprised.

"Hello," I began. "I noticed your . . . door, and I thought, well, perhaps you might be able to help me."

He stared at me in confusion, and I realized he might not even know what I was saying. "I'm sorry. Do you speak English?"

"Of course," the young man answered in a thick Indian accent.

"Well, I saw your LA Lakers door, and well, I'm visiting from LA, and I was hoping you might be able to help me."

"Ellll, ahhhhh?" the man drew out the letters.

"Yes, and—" I tried to continue.

"Kooooh-beeeee," he interrupted.

"Yes, yes, Kobe Bryant. I mean, I'm not Kobe Bryant, but I have been to a game, and . . . well, you see I am in a bit of a bind. I was left here by some man, and to be honest, I don't really know what's going on."

The man's smile broadened even further before he uttered the words I needed to hear so badly, "Welcome home, Koooh-beee!"

Welcome home. As I soon found out, the Lakers fan in front of me was a recently graduated university student who had come to Delhi to find work in the tech industry. Sankar had left his family and his home near the Kashmir border in order to pursue a dream of success in the big city. Instead, he had found work in the back of a restaurant and a new home in the small shanty that he shared with a coworker in the heart of the Delhi slum.

Sankar didn't have to work until the evening, so he took it upon himself to be my tour guide for the day, taking me to meet his cousin, another immigrant to this Delhi life, who had come from the rural south in the hopes of attaining his dream of being a chemist. Shiva was married, and as his wife prepared us a hearty lunch filled with rice and curries, I told them how I had ended up at Sankar's home—with no shoes or shirt and nothing to eat. Sankar and his cousins laughed as I shared my story, nearly crying at the fact that I had agreed to such a ridiculous venture.

"You gave the man your shoes?" Shiva asked through his laughter.

"Well, yes," I replied, beginning to realize how ridiculous all this was. Why would I give up my easy American life to be left half-naked in Delhi?

Finally, I realized, "I guess it was so I could meet you."

After lunch, Sankar took me to play cricket with a group of children in a trash-filled field down the road. The sun was beginning to fall in the sky as the hollers and laughter of the cricket game echoed across the slum. I had been so caught up in my day with Sankar, I had nearly forgotten about Naasih. I had started the morning in fear and exhaustion, caught up in what I couldn't control, but I was ending the day connected to something much larger.

I don't know how much you know about professional tight-rope walkers, but most of them do not practice on calm, low-wind days. No, most try to get out there when the weather's rough, when the wind is blowing, and every step forces them to at once tense and relax their muscles along the line. It's by handing their fates over to chaos that they find the balance to walk through it.

Always pay attention.

After the game, Sankar and I walked to Rata Road, where Naasih had left me. We shook hands.

"You tell Kobe he has big fan in Delhi. He come visit some time," he suggested.

"If I ever meet him, Sankar. I'll be sure to let him know." As I watched him walk away, I could hear a slight chuckle coming from behind me. There stood Naasih, like Obi-Wan Kenobi, waiting and watching from a quiet distance. As we wound our way out of the slums, he said, "You're glowing, Leon."

Not really the kind of compliment a man wants to receive, but I understood. I was glowing. I had been knocked entirely off balance and out of my comfort zone, and I felt that wild burst of life that had been so sorely missing from my own.

How Can You Throw Yourself Off Balance?

Now, I know not everyone can—or should—be left to fend for themselves in a Delhi slum, but we all have things we can do in our own lives to throw us off balance. Maybe it's taking a yoga class. Hell, maybe it's taking a tightrope class. Maybe it's going to your estranged sister's wedding, or calling your father, or asking for a raise at work. Write down three things that sound incredibly uncomfortable to you, and pick one to actually do:

1. _____
_____
_____
_____

2. _____
_____
_____
_____

3. _____
_____
_____
_____

TURNING BOREDOM INTO MAGIC

Over the next few weeks, Naasih had me stand on a sidewalk in Kolkata and scream like a madman. He took me on a train across India, and had me ask others for food. He led me through bat caves and a forest of banyan trees, and across the mismatched patterns of the Indian landscape, offering me stories of his own experiences, and often just the silence of experiencing life. As he explained to me during our second week, "This journey isn't about me, Leon. It's about you. This journey is about watching how the world can change us if we're willing to let it."

On most days, I could see those changes taking place. That passionate curiosity that I had lost in Los Angeles was reignited in the dirty, colorful, crowded, magnificent places to which Naasih had led me. But then I woke up in Shirdi, sleeping on a cot in a cockroach-infested room, and all that beautiful enlightenment seemed to evaporate. Once again, I seemed to take one step back, moving away from the magic of life's possibilities and into the fear that everything would surely go wrong.

I could easily blame the gastrointestinal issues I was having. As I quickly discovered, my British belly had some trouble with the Indian delights. But what was happening in my gut was also a reflection of what was happening in my soul. I was being exorcised of everything I had come to believe about life. And that process was way more exhausting than any kind of stomach trouble. Like most animals when they feel threatened,

I just wanted to go home and curl up in the safety of the life I had known before.

And then that morning in Shirdi, Naasih told me to get up, "We're going to meet a living saint."

The only thing I could muster was: "Sounds boring."

I received an icy stare in return. I guess by week three, Naasih thought I should have known better, and the truth was, I did. Too often in life we try to avoid the quieter inner work by being active on the outside. We're so busy *doing* that we don't have time to stop and question how we are *being* in life. I had begun to recognize this while in India. I was no longer a set of stories and belief systems passed on by others. I was absolutely free to be me. But on that morning, getting more sleep still sounded better than meeting a saint. We checked out of our hotel (if that is what you could call it), and drove several hours to the ashram. Our taxi moved through the chain-link fence and onto a large property overgrown with weeds and palm trees. It didn't feel very enlightened.

"So where are all the saints?" I jokingly mumbled.

Naasih didn't say anything, finally offering as we began to pull up to the decrepit white building, "This is a silent ashram."

"Sooo . . ." I began.

"No one speaks."

"No one?"

He gave me that icy stare again. "No one."

We entered a large and crumbling hall where there were hundreds of children meditating. Four adults were sitting cross-legged on a raised platform at the front. "I wonder if any of these chaps are the saints," I mused, silently, for obvious reasons, quickly concluding that these four people couldn't possibly be saints. I mean there were no glowing auras shining above their heads. No chirping of birds.

Find your authentic purpose.

I sat with Naasih, who bowed his head, and I followed suit. Suddenly, my mind was louder than it had been on the whole trip. The silence that had seemed to permeate my Indian existence flew right out the window, and the hum of anxiety that had besieged my life in LA quickly returned. What was I doing on this trip? What was I doing with my life? What would I do when I got home? What if I never got home? My thoughts beat against the insides of my head as I felt my pulse rise to greet them. That old doubt began to bubble up in me—the one that said, "Nothing good can come from this. And nothing will ever change." I felt as though I were going to be trapped in that ashram for eternity, with nothing to do and no one to talk to. I was suddenly convinced that Naasih was going to leave me there. I had failed the test, and now I was going to repent (in silence!) for the rest of my life.

After the longest hour of my life, the meditation ended, and we were ushered into a small room where one of the men who had been at the front of the large hall was sitting on a small carpet, cross-legged. Naasih nodded toward him, clearly not needing words to show me that this was indeed the saint. This is why we had slept in a bug-infested room. This is why we had driven four hours with no air-conditioning on a death-defying road. I was sick and exhausted. And I was not impressed.

I was led before the man, whom I would later learn was called Yogiraj. Four other men, including Naasih, sat with me as we bowed our heads in silence. And then I saw it. The halo? The golden aura? No, I saw the still and blissful face of God transfixed upon Yogiraj. Suddenly the silence seemed like the sweetest nectar I had ever drunk. It was as though Yogiraj had been made from the same fabric as Jesus or Buddha or Mohammed. As though the spirit had been made flesh, and everything I ever believed or didn't believe failed to mean anything against the light of this man's love. I didn't want to ever leave. I looked at Yogiraj's face as all my doubts began to fade away. All I knew was that I was experiencing a miracle. Boredom, or what I thought was boredom, stood tantalizingly close to magic, and suddenly, I found myself willing to become the change.

When I closed my eyes, I could still feel the powerful presence of the man sitting before me. It was as though I was experiencing bliss through his eyes. Not the kind of bliss from going out and buying more and doing more, but the kind of bliss that could only result from *becoming* more, myself—becoming who I was truly meant to be. And I knew, without even looking around, that everyone in that room was having the same experience.

As Naasih and I drove back to our hotel, he told me that Yogiraj's presence simply reflected our true selves. "You see, Leon, the self gets lost in this frenetic world—in all the talking, the thinking about what smart and witty thing we're going to say next, how we're going to respond. Isn't it funny that whenever we get bored, we get anxious? We know that there is more to life. We feel that restless spirit pulsing inside of us, and yet we do nothing to let it dance. Instead, we sink into that darkness."

"That's why I didn't want to leave the hotel."

"Yes, I know," Naasih smiled. "Your stomach hurt. You were tired. It was understandable, but we become immersed in the lie that what's important is the physical matter around us, and we forget that really, the only thing that matters is the spirit inside. When we take care of the spirit, the rest usually follows."

Feel deeply; feel others.

"It's that moment, right?" I practically shouted, my energy bounding around the back of the taxi. "That moment, when we think we can no longer live in our skin that we finally are willing to shed it."

"I think you might actually be learning something on this trip," Naasih laughed.

Can You Recognize Miracles?

Now, it's your turn. Where are the miracles in your life today? They don't need to derive from the silence of a saint in an Indian ashram, of course. They can just as easily be in the love for your dog (or rather the fact that your dog loves you), the kindness of a stranger on a bad day, or perhaps something bigger—a new love, a new job, a new child. They can be as simple as spotting a deer while driving to work in the morning. Name three moments where you saw the magic in the everyday and/or three people who have made you believe that such magic is possible:

1. _____

_____

_____

_____

_____

2. _____

_____

_____

_____

3. _____

_____

_____

_____

"I am taking you to see a living saint," he said.

"Sounds boring," I said.

Indeed.

SHARE YOUR GIFTS

A few days later, Naasih gave me my itinerary. I was heading home to LA, and the journey would take me thirty-seven hours. Yes, you heard that right. I would be making my way westward through Delhi, Dubai, London, and Los Angeles. And I would be going home alone. Naasih was staying behind.

"What's this?" I asked, looking down at the flight schedule.

Naasih smiled that patient smile, "It's your chance to give back. On every layover, I want you to tell people about your journey. I want you to share these stories with others.

"Share your inner gifts, Leon," Naasih explained. "Money, things, accomplishments—these are all wonderful luxuries, but they are not what is important. It is our stories that enrich us, that help us grow, that teach others how to grow, too."

As I traveled through the cities on my itinerary, I realized that I couldn't share anything with anyone as long as I was stuck in my comfort zone. Over the next two days, I regaled people with my crazy adventures, and I built connections. I don't know if, afterward, anyone called up Naasih looking to book a trip, but I do know that they all couldn't help but wonder what it might be like. What it would be like to let go of everything we think we know, and discover, instead, what is lying inside us?

What Gifts Can You Share?

We all have gifts to share. For me, it was telling my story. When I got home from that trip with Naasih, I started to write the first pages of my first book, *Amazing Adventures of a Nobody*. What are your gifts and how could you start sharing them? Maybe you like playing football and could volunteer to coach a local team. Maybe you play the guitar and could start performing at a nearby open mic. Gandhi once said, "In a gentle way, you can shake the world." Though my trip to India was by no means gentle, it showed me that sometimes all it takes is one yes to shake up your entire world. What can you do today to share your gifts with the world?

_____

_____

_____

_____

_____

_____

_____

_____

Sometimes, we have to jump out of that hot tub and into the chaos, changing our habits and routines without really understanding the consequences of those changes. We have to confront the reality that our comfort zone is a lie, and we have to take on discomfort and imbalance in order to shed those fears that keep us from being who we were meant to be. We have to be willing to accept that we will—frequently—take one step back on the journey. We must be willing to shake the world. Otherwise, how will we know we're alive?

FOUR

THE WAY OF THE STUDENT

"Don't let your learning lead to knowledge. Let your learning lead to action."

—JIM ROHN

"Leon?" I could hear the voice calling from far away, but I wasn't sure where it was coming from.

"Leon." I was busy daydreaming about being a professional footballer on the verge of winning a big game. Sometimes I would be in the trenches of World War I, fighting for queen and country. I would always magically miss being hit by the hail of bullets coming my way.

"Leon!" And then there I was, back in class, the teacher growling at me from across the classroom.

Mrs. Davies waited until I came back fully into the room.

"Can you tell the class what the importance of the Magna Carta is?"

The eyes of the classroom were on me. It felt like no one was taking a breath.

"The Mag—" I slowly began.

"The Magna Carta, Leon. We have been discussing it for much of this class."

The room continued to stare as I shrugged and waited for the teacher to move on. I was used to shrugging and waiting for the teacher to move on. It was the modus operandi of my academic career.

And why I hated school. I didn't want to be sitting in class, memorizing books, and repeating the information back to my teachers. I wanted to be out in the world, or as I often did in my childhood, imagining myself in some magical, far-off place.

It wasn't until much later that I realized just how much I loved learning. Walking through the ruins of a long-lost civilization while seeing and touching the relics of a bygone era, tracing the footsteps of our ancestors, feeling how they lived, experiencing what they experienced—now, that was learning. Having made my way across the globe, I feel I have finally received the education I failed to get in school. I have witnessed or experienced wonders of nature and science that never touched me back in biology class. I have had to calculate speed, velocity, distance, and time in ways that failed to mean anything to me in math. If a bus is going at sixty miles an hour across four hundred miles, can you get to Bangkok for a 6:00 a.m. flight? That would have gone right over my head in school, but not while sitting on a bus going through Thailand, hand gripping my plane ticket.

But perhaps most importantly, traveling has enabled me to see how history informs the future.

I remember once walking along the wall that separates Israel and the Palestinian territories. On either side of that wall were two groups of people at war with one another and yet both were practicing the same thing: their faith.

With every trip, I have learned something new. And further, each of those lessons informs my future. Because as long as we are learning, changing, growing, and discovering who exactly we are in a world filled with so many stories, the world around us is the greatest classroom of all. And all we have to do to become a part of it is leave home.

Don't judge others unless you're willing to judge yourself.

As much as schools, television, and the Internet can teach us about the world beyond our living rooms, the only way to really be a student of this world, is to become a part of it. Salman Rushdie once wrote, "To understand just one life, you have to swallow the world."

Whether it's taking a trip to the Roman Forum, standing in reverence at the Normandy beaches, or going to a series of readings at your local library, world lessons are always beckoning us. We don't have to go far to learn. Just asking a stranger about their life could open us up to a lesson we might not have even known we needed to learn.

There are three places that have changed the very fabric of who I am today: Auschwitz, Bhutan, and the British Library in London.

LEARNING FROM OUR PAST

Approximately thirty miles from Krakow is the Auschwitz concentration camp. I was traveling through Europe a couple of years ago and decided that, at the age of thirty-five, it was time for me to visit the site of one of mankind's greatest tragedies. As I drove up to the imposing prison, I was overwhelmed by the stories I had heard of its horrors. Images I had seen of gaunt survivors tentatively walking out of its gates flashed through my mind.

I walked under the infamous gate, with its cruel greeting: *Arbeit macht frei* (Work will set you free). I had read books about this place and watched movies set there, but no amount of mass media can capture the horror of what really happened in the prison camps of Nazi Germany—the lives that were brutally extinguished, children ripped from mothers, fathers carelessly killed, more than six million people murdered because they were considered "other."

Sadly, many people still perpetrate this thinking in our world. Genocide did not end in 1945. And on a far, far lesser scale, the cruelties that men (and women) visit upon each other can be seen each day around us.

How often have we judged people because they didn't look like us or pray like us or think like us? How often have we been judged?

As I walked along the wide dirt pathways between the buildings of Auschwitz, I could feel the ghosts of its past walking beside me. The stories of the millions of children, women, and men who died there echoed from the otherwise utilitarian rows of buildings that stand as a reminder of what terrible deeds men can do. Inside the buildings, the walls were lined with

Give your sorrow a voice.

photos of prisoners—lawyers and doctors, housewives and students. They weren't "other." They were people. People living normal lives, going to work, reading books, holding their children at night, and then one day, their perfectly normal lives changed forever. They were stripped of their belongings and wrenched from their families. They were taken to camps like Auschwitz, where their photos were taken, their heads were shaved, and they lived on the bitter side of survival until they were either murdered or freed, having to learn how to valiantly live again.

I visited the gas chambers. I walked through the barracks, with their wood-and-hay beds. I saw the communal toilets, where privacy simply didn't exist. I passed the large, barren rooms filled with human hair, with shoes, with suitcases, with the remnants of the people who learned what happens when fear of the "other" leads to murder.

Of course, I had known the facts before driving up that day. I had known the number: six million. I had known about the gas chambers. I had even known about the hair. But knowing something, knowing facts, and experiencing history—or at least being close enough to reach out and touch the artifacts of history—are two completely different things.

Far too often, we allow the TV or the computer to educate us. We think because we've been told the story or read about it, we know the story. Unfortunately, it's why history far too often repeats itself. Because knowing something very rarely changes us. It takes experience to produce the elements of compassion, of understanding, of change. Visiting Auschwitz is a deep and powerful reminder of what took place in those brutal years of Nazi Germany.

Many have said that if everyone in the world visited Auschwitz, genocide would be wiped from our vocabulary. I am not sure such a profound outcome is possible, but I know we would all be far more sensitive and compassionate creatures for seeing it.

After World War II, people began to say, "Never forget." Meaning, never let these horrors happen again. But I believe "Never forget" can also refer to never forgetting the beauty of your own life, right now.

Never forget to cherish every precious moment of freedom. Because the small disasters that affect our lives are nothing in relation to the horrors the prisoners of Auschwitz had to live and many people still experience today. But on the other side of that darkness is an incandescent light. Although two-thirds of the Jewish population in Europe was murdered in those concentration camps, one-third survived. They survived. They went on to create new families. They worked again. They achieved success. They found love. They got another chance at life.

I might have left Auschwitz on that cloudy afternoon in July, but Auschwitz did not leave me. This is what true learning is about. It demands we remember. Facts from a book can fall away once the last page is read, but the memory of an experience can linger forever. Auschwitz demanded that I live that experience. How could I take in the darkest parts of human experience and still find some light? How could I ignore the fact that every day I was lucky enough to be alive, to be free? I couldn't.

Where Can You Visit the Past?

What can you learn from history today? Is it your time to visit Auschwitz? Or does your hometown offer lessons from its past?

Though my education has taken me to far-flung places, sometimes our best lessons can be found in our own backyards. It's up to us to find them. What is one place you could make a plan to visit today? Write it down, and then make that plan a reality. If you can go today, go today. If not, start putting the wheels in motion to go out and greet the past.

_____

_____

_____

_____

_____

_____

_____

LESSONS FROM THE FUTURE

When we lead with our heads, we become focused on competition: do more, earn more, make more. But when we lead with our hearts, we learn how to collaborate. How can we work better together? How can we help one another more? How can we love more, be more joyous, be more, period?

Unfortunately, in most modern societies, we are expected to lead with our heads, leaving our hearts to beg from behind. But have you ever had the experience of leading with your heart? Have you ever helped another person without expecting something in return? Maybe it was as simple as helping someone cross the street. Maybe it was a larger gesture, like volunteering your time. Maybe it was helping someone find a new way of life, or helping them get back on their feet. Kindness often starts in small acts, but it grows exponentially, changing our behaviors, and pushing us to find ways in which we can always be helping others. Because the more we are of service, the more we are in joy. Give to others, and you shall find. This is why, when I heard that the tiny nation of Bhutan had created something called the Gross National Happiness index, I had to find out more.

Love is a way of life.

Bhutan is not a perfect place. Pretty far from it. But in 1972, its fourth Dragon King, Jigme Singye Wangchuck, decided there was something more important to the success of his country than economics. He felt that the country's greatest domestic product was actually the happiness of its citizens. Though the fourth Dragon King has been long succeeded by the fifth, the concept of Gross National Happiness has spread across the world, inspiring similar measurements of well-being in countries like Thailand and the United Kingdom, and in organizations like the John F. Kennedy School of Government at Harvard and the Organization for Economic Co-operation and Development (OECD), which launched the "Better Life Index" in 2011. In 2013, even Seattle got on board with their Social Progress Index, which was inspired by Bhutan's GNH.

King Jigme Singye Wangchuck decided to create a measurement of success that is not based solely on gross domestic product (GDP) or income. He wanted to create a society where happiness is just as important a resource as the US dollar or the NASDAQ index. The king and his advisors determined that Gross National Happiness had four pillars: the promotion of equitable and sustainable socioeconomic development; preservation and promotion of cultural values; conservation of the natural environment; and establishment of good governance.

They decided they would measure their country's wealth through the happiness of their people. They decided to lead from their hearts.

I reached out to their press office, hoping to meet someone from their ministry and learn more about Gross National Happiness (GNH). To my surprise, someone wrote me back, and an interview was set.

In the days leading up to my trip, I began to question the notion of GNH. As much as it sounded kind in theory, I cynically wondered what the real motive was. Were they just using this concept to increase tourism, to get more people to know who they were? Surely, no one would celebrate happiness just for the sake of happiness.

When I settled into my seat at the government offices in Thimpu, the capital of Bhutan, I couldn't help but share my theory with the Minister of the Environment, the man who had agreed to meet with me.

"So, has GNH been a boost to your tourism?" I asked, trying to frame my questions innocently.

"No," the minister smiled, sensing my cynicism, "We do not get anything from the policy."

"But surely, more people want to see it in action."

"I would think so, too," he replied in his best English. "But a lot of people don't know what to do with happiness. A lot of people are more comfortable to complain. It's easy to see the problem in life. It's harder sometimes to let us see joy."

I understood. It is harder sometimes to let us see joy. It's easier to look at the day before you and recognize what needs to change. We are less quick to honor what we already have.

More often than not, we see the darker side of things. We nitpick at our loved ones, swimming in a dirty pond of pessimism rather than in the vast ocean of optimism. Years ago, I was traveling on the Trans-Siberian Railway from Mongolia to Beijing, and ended up rooming with a Dutch psychotherapist in one of the train's sleeper cars.

As we began to talk, I asked why I struggled so much to see the beauty of the world, even as it was right there, just outside the train window.

"Cavemen," was his one-word reply. As the icy landscape swept past, he explained that we were hardwired to be negative. Back when we were cavemen, we were at risk of being eaten by a saber-toothed tiger pretty much every day. We had to constantly be on the lookout for signs of danger. That pessimistic attitude saved our lives. And our need to collect and hoard and always worry about how much we have or don't have? It comes from the same

Embrace the resistance.

place. If cavemen hadn't planned and protected their resources, they would have starved themselves to extinction. But do we really need to keep acting like cavemen?

The minister explained that officials in Bhutan hadn't been thinking about quarterly earnings when the king came up with the policy, they were thinking about the long-term.

"We hope one day everyone will have a GNH index," he added. "One day, we might all stop looking so hard at how many dollars we have in the bank and more on the joy we have here." He held his hand to his heart for a moment, and I couldn't help but imitate the gesture. Why don't I stop more and feel that? Why don't we all take the time in our days to place our hands to our hearts and feel the joy that lies inside? Probably because we're too busy going online to check how much money we have in the bank. But isn't wealth supposed to bring us joy?

"We think that money, it brings the happiness," the minister explained. "But what if we just experienced the happiness for free?"

He stopped for a moment and let the words sit with me before continuing, "This is the future Bhutan sees. This is the future for all."

This is the Way of the Traveler. Because if we go out into the world from a place of love, then our potential to engage with it becomes unlimited. We are able to e-mail foreign government ministers and ask for an interview. We are able to approach a stranger on the street and ask for help. We are able to contribute to that Gross National Happiness index in ways that rival the NASDAQ. We don't need loads of money or fancy degrees to become investors in the world around us. We just need to connect with the rich fabric of humanity at every turn, joining in its joy, and when we can, alleviating its sorrow.

As I went out into Bhutan to experience its culture and meet its people, I kept placing that hand over my heart, and pausing to feel the joy inside. And that joy was reflected in everyone I met.

That's not to say that every person I encountered was happy. As the Minister explained to me that day, "Gross National Happiness is not a promise of happiness, but rather about creating the conditions for happiness."

After leaving the minister's office, I drove through the majestic hills of Bhutan on the little yellow motorcycle I had been driving across the world (but more on that soon). I weaved my way through the mist-filled countryside and through the small villages that dotted its landscape. I had been traveling all day. I had been traveling for months. I was exhausted, and looking for a place to rest. Finally, I found myself at a small farmhouse one hundred twisting miles out from Thimpu. I spoke with an older farmer in his field, and he directed me to his son, Bikash. As I quickly discovered, almost everyone under the age of forty in Bhutan speaks English because it is taught in school.

Bikash was standing in the doorway of his house when I saw him. He was wearing blue jeans and a hooded sweatshirt, but he was sweaty from work, and had a line of soil smeared across his forehead. He had cropped black hair and slim shoulders that didn't seem broad enough for the heavy work of farm life.

I drove up and waved. Bikash waved back as though he had been expecting me. The truth is we had never met. I got off my motorcycle as this modern-day farmer approached me.

After I told him about my quest to see the government policy in action, Bikash immediately invited me inside for some tea. We shared a bit of our stories, and I explained more of why I was there, how I had ended up in Bhutan, yet again searching for an answer that seemed to elude me.

"I thought maybe Gross National Happiness would be that answer," I explained.

Bikash smiled broadly, as though I had just brought up his favorite football team. "Different people have different opinions about Gross National Happiness. For me, it's being at home with my family, having three meals in a day. My family is happy. This means happiness to me."

"So happiness equals simplicity?" I asked.

"Yes, exactly," he replied.

"We should tell the rest of the world that."

"Yes, we should," Bikash laughed.

While leaving Bikash's home, I thought about the joys of simplicity, about the conditions for happiness. As I drove through Bhutan, I began to realize that those conditions were what produced joy. Not the expectations of how things can or should be different. Now, does that mean we pack away the big dream and just accept life as it is? No, change and acceptance can happen simultaneously. We can see where our lives can be better, how our dreams can be more fulfilled, and still appreciate the simple joys of our present lives. We can set up the conditions for our own happiness, both for today and for tomorrow.

As I continued my journey, I wondered, could this be our future? Could this vision of collaboration and community really replace the fast-paced, money-driven world we live in today?

Maybe we are evolving past negativity and fear. Maybe we will finally accept that we have enough. That we're going to be okay. That competition is only keeping us in a cave. And that collaboration is the way of the future.

I left Bhutan a different man, and not just because of the concept of Gross National Happiness, but also because of the people who embodied it. I had seen what can happen when you stop and feel the joy in your heart, when you make a conscious choice to leave behind that caveman brain and live from a far more evolved place. As I sat with Bikash that afternoon, it wasn't about whose country did things better, or who came from a better place, it was about two people connecting through their hearts, united by a common hope that we would all one day evolve to a place where kindness would be the common currency.

When I returned home, I knew that I was going to do things differently. For a number of months I had been trying to sell a TV project about that trip around the world, without success.

So I decided to find someone else's project to invest in instead, to offer someone else the chance that I had failed to find for myself. It was a small independent movie that Steve was working on. This time I didn't need to ask a client to invest in the project; I became the investor. And you know what happened? That movie turned into a bigger success than the one I had envisioned for my own project.

Even now, when I find myself wondering how I am doing, all I have to do is put my hand on my heart. And then I pause and feel what emotions are turning in there.

How Can You Create the Conditions for Happiness?

We can all create the conditions for our own happiness, but first we must determine what stops us from experiencing joy. Put your hand over your heart. What do you feel there? Sorrow? Disappointment? Or do you right now feel excitement and joy? What spins around in that mysterious place beneath your palm?

And what do you wish you felt more of? Write down two choices that you can make in order to raise your Gross Happiness Index. Maybe it's going out and getting a massage once a week. Maybe it's joining a local sports team. Maybe it's spending more time with your family. What can you do to start leading from the heart?

1. _____

_____

_____

_____

_____

_____

2. _____

_____

_____

_____

_____

LEARNING FROM THE PRESENT

Learning from the world around us doesn't always demand that we buy a plane ticket. In fact, some of the biggest lessons happen in our own backyards. For many years, my backyard was London. Growing up in the rainy city, I prided myself on being a city boy. The only thing was that I never really enjoyed doing city activities. Going to museums? Not really. Seeing plays? That's okay. Checking out the library? I'll pass. I grew up in a city filled with art and culture, but for all my city-boy pride, I just wanted to get out. But then I met Lydia.

Lydia had also grown up in London. But unlike me, she loved what our city had to offer. She went to local plays, and would go to small quartets in the park. She knew the big museums like the back of her hand. She loved libraries and art galleries and cafés that I frequently passed and always felt intimidated to enter. She knew the difference between a countertenor and a mezzo-soprano. At the time, I was in my early twenties, and I wasn't as interested in these local locales. But I was interested in Lydia.

> The depth
> of your
> being is
> where the
> magic lies.

I've been through enough therapy to know I have commitment issues. Maybe it's why I have shied away from the title of teacher. How can I offer anyone anything when I am flawed? When I make mistakes? When I can't get my love life straight? But the truth is that every person I have fallen in love with has taught me something. Some were great teachers about the world. Others taught me most about the world within. Lydia did both.

Together, we explored London. I became a tourist in my own town. I went to operas, art galleries, and cafés, and they ceased to intimidate me. I fell in love with the British Museum, and I fell in love with Lydia. She wasn't afraid of anything or anyone. And she loved the world with an intensity that proved it. When I asked why she loved London so much, she explained, "Because I feel it's the one city that's caught smack-dab in the middle of the past and the future. Look around,

Leon—we could be in the 1800s, or we could just easily be in the next century, which I guess makes London all about the present. It's halfway between yesterday and tomorrow."

Lydia lived in the present, and by her side, so did I. I was a few years into that finance career I complained about so much, but suddenly that was just my day job. My true passion was exploring the city of my childhood. I explained to Lydia that though I was proud of my city, it also reminded me of the years growing up there, years that were filled with torment.

"I hated school," I confessed. "The teachers were just as bad as the bullies. Both made fun of me."

I told her the story of the Magna Carta, and how later in that same week, Mrs. Davies asked me, "I know you come from a good family, so what is wrong with you?"

"What was wrong with me?" was a question I had been asking since.

One morning, Lydia told me she wanted to take me somewhere we hadn't been.

She smiled proudly, "The British Library."

Now for all of Lydia's great tours of the city, the British Library didn't sound like the best of them.

And what was worse was that, by that point, I was beginning to think maybe Lydia and I weren't doing so well, either. Like in many of my relationships, the initial spark was beginning to dull. After just three months, I was beginning to run out of things to say, and I wondered when Lydia and I would start going longer and longer between phone calls and dates.

As I was beginning to realize, people can fall out of love just as quickly as they fall into it. But I agreed to go to the library because I'm the kind of guy who has trouble saying no.

Lydia was visibly excited by the time we made it to the library. I thought she might be losing her mind, but then she led me into a quiet room, trying her best to whisper, "Look."

And there it was. The Magna Carta.

I'm not sure if you remember that particular lesson in school, but the Magna Carta was the document King John signed in 1215 that guaranteed that man should live free, without fear of prosecution or imprisonment. It was one of the first human rights documents on the planet. A basic contract that stated horrors like Nazi Germany could not be committed. That man had the right to be free.

I walked around, reading about the document and its history. I also read about its effects since its creation, about how many of the world's greatest constitutions probably wouldn't exist without it.

> Without a foundation, the wind will blow you away.

Lydia walked up to me and said, "See, now you'll never not know what the Magna Carta is."

I laughed, "I wish Mrs. Davies took us here."

Suddenly, Lydia's face grew dark. "I think it's important for all men and women to be free."

"Of course," I began.

But she interrupted me. "I think it's better if you and I are free."

All of a sudden I realized Lydia was breaking up with me. In front of the Magna Carta. At the British Library.

"Are you sure?" I asked, suddenly feeling like our recent lull could be overcome.

"Sometimes, Leon, people are just meant for right now. Not for the future. One day, we'll both meet the person who will land themselves in our futures, but I'd rather you and I just leave it, knowing we enjoyed the present."

She looked back at the Magna Carta, "I think it's better that way."

Later, I would sometimes see Lydia at the cafés she had introduced me to. We would run into each other at the art galleries. And then, five years ago, a mutual friend e-mailed me to let me know Lydia had passed away.

"Cancer," was his heartbreaking explanation.

"But she asked people not to mourn," he wrote. "She said she had lived more lifetimes in thirty years than most people do in a century."

Lydia had forever changed me, but I was almost equally altered by her death. When I logged off the computer that day, it felt like the sound had been drained from the world. I walked outside, and there were no birds, no whistle in the wind. It was shocking and horrible and unbelievably sad.

But then as my heart began to accept the truth, I heard a

deep hum from the world. It was as if the whole earth were pre-paring to break into song. I sat down and began to cry. They were tears of sadness, but also tears of joy. I was overwhelmed with my incredible luck that in all the lifetimes of this world, I had the chance to meet Lydia.

Lydia never traveled to far-off lands. She didn't need to. She learned everything she wanted of the world from the city she had been born in, and she shared her knowledge with others. She knew that in order to stay truly present, she had to be willing to give it away. Going out and seeing things doesn't necessarily mean crossing oceans or getting on planes. History is available to us all. The wonders of humanity reside in every town.

Most of all, we learn from those who stand firmly rooted in the present, living their lives with passion and gusto. There are so many ways to always be learning. Whether it's through taking a class or starting a conversation, going on a trip or talking to a random stranger, the point of education is not to memorize facts, but to awaken our curiosity, the ever-lingering question of our purpose. It's from the beauty and tragedy of that answer that we become transformed. If we stay in one place, we stagnate. We get trapped by one viewpoint, one be-lief system, one pair of glasses, and we miss the kaleidoscope of experiences waiting for us outside.

How Can You Become a Teacher?

Most of us have had a Lydia in our life. But the question is, who can you be a Lydia for today? Perhaps it's simply taking your sister to the museum, or your child to work. Maybe it's booking a trip to Rome with your wife, or taking a road trip to New Mexico with your best friend. Who can you reach out to, and say, "I want to show you the world outside my door. I want to be present for this life." Name one person to whom you can be a teacher, and then decide how you will show them a bit more of your world, or the great world around us.

_____

_____

_____

_____

_____

_____

_____

_____

From the tragedy of Auschwitz to the joyful hearts of the Bhutanese, this world has broken me open over and over again. But it's the people who do the biggest number on us, who forever change who we are and how we look at the world.

FIVE

THE WAY TO CONNECT COMES THROUGH DISCONNECTING

"Your heart and my heart are very, very old friends."

—HAFIZ

Have you ever seen the movie *Zorba the Greek*? Probably not, huh? Most people haven't, so I'll tell you a little bit about it (spoiler alert!). The movie, and the book on which it was based, is about a Brit of Greek descent named Basil who gives up his corporate life in London (sound familiar?) to seek adventure and start a new business on a Greek island. While traveling through his parents' homeland, he meets a local named Zorba. Zorba does not live in Basil's buttoned-down, financial-statements world. Zorba lives free—so free that he at once terrifies and inspires Basil, setting off a chain of events that Basil cannot control as he learns to live again. Oh, and they dance, the film ending with Zorba teaching Basil to dance with abandon on a deserted Greek beach. There, now you don't have to watch it yourself. I saw this movie for the first time in my mid-twenties, and it was like watching the film version of my life.

So many of us live life like Basil: bored, tired, scared. We know there are beaches out there we should be dancing upon, but we can't seem to break out of our well-worn routines to find them. We find ourselves caught in the survival game. We have bills to pay, and families to take care of. Even if we're just starting out in life, we feel the heavy weight of that word— responsibility—and we forgo the abandoned beach, even when it's down the street. We give up on the idea of adventure, thinking it is available only to the people who identify themselves as "adventurers."

> Allow greatness to flow through you.

In the film, Zorba tells his suited protégé, "There is something missing in you, boss. A touch of madness! Unless you cut the string, you will never really live."

When I first heard this quote, it touched a raw nerve. I was not living my life. I was not *being*. I was not indulging in that touch of madness. I was holding on for dear life, and it was costing me mine. I was attached to my cell phone, addicted to my e-mail, and incapable of thinking I could ever live a life that didn't run by a strictly set and closely followed calendar.

And I am not alone.

So many of us find ourselves confined by the gadgets and routines and accoutrements of modern life that we think should free us. Sure, the Internet is basically the whole of the world's knowledge at the tips of our fingers, but sometimes it also prevents us from being present in the world around us. Sometimes, in order to connect with the world, we need to cut the cord to all the e-mails and updates and newsfeeds—the unending, digital responsibility. Sometimes we need to break up the routine, put down the phone, and just go live.

Where in your life, today, are you behaving like Basil? How are you allowing the responsibilities and routines of your buttoned-down life to stop you from living adventurously? Instead of answering a work e-mail, spend some time with a family member. Instead of ordering Chinese takeout online, go to your local Chinatown and try a new restaurant. How can you cut the string today, and embrace the madness instead?

Like Basil, my life had turned into a black-and-white movie, but the worst part was the fact that I was writing and directing it. My need to be perfect stemmed from my deepest fears of being imperfect. On the outside, it looked like I had everything together: I was twenty-five and had a good job, a nice apartment, a pretty girlfriend. On the inside, I couldn't help but feel like a fraud. Because I was a fraud. I hated the job. I was ungrateful for the apartment. I was a jerk to the girlfriend. And

I went to the bars at night to avoid all three. I chose to drink away my reality, instead of changing it.

Though it took me quite a few more years before I was willing to actually do anything about it, those words from *Zorba the Greek* haunted me: "There is something missing in you, boss. A touch of madness! Unless you cut the string, you will never really live."

Fast-forward nearly ten years, and so many things had changed: I was living in America, I was working in TV, and I had made so many dreams come true. Yet I began to feel the black-and-white seeping into my life. Once again, I was gripping everything so tightly that there were claw marks all over the place. I was one guy at work. I was one guy at home. And though my days at the bar were long over, I was in yet another relationship where I just couldn't be present. The worst part: I was telling everyone else what they were doing wrong, but had once again stopped looking at myself. I had stopped laughing, but perhaps worse than that, I had stopped dancing. I had once again become Basil, but I decided it was time for me to become Zorba.

So much of our lives is about connecting, but I had begun to connect to the wrong things. I was connected to work, but not to my coworkers. Sure, I asked about their weekends. We talked about the traffic (as you do when you live in Los Angeles) and whatever the hot topic was that week on the Internet. We complained, a lot. But we weren't sharing anything about our true lives. About the fight we had with our significant others, the fear we had about our mothers' health, the moment we held our baby daughter and our eyes filled with tears of joy. We were living side by side, but not in relationships with one another. We were living with the light of the screen on our faces, and not the light of the sun.

So I decided to do what anyone would do in that situation. I decided to buy a vintage London taxi and drive across America, offering free rides to people along the way. Because, well, why not? I wanted to feel connected with the world again, and I wanted to do it in ways that I was failing to do in Los Angeles. Because the Way of the Traveler shows us that in order to connect, we must first disconnect from the systems and smartphones that block us from one another.

Where are you frozen?

I knew what I was going to do; all I had to do was find a vintage London taxi in America. How hard could that be? I did what any of us would do: I went on the Internet. Because though disconnecting ourselves from our gadgets is the first way to connect with the people around us, I also recognize the Internet can be one of the greatest assets to adventure. One click can lead us anywhere from a local museum to a different country. And on the Internet, we can find the resources to make our dreams come true. So when I decided I wanted to buy a vintage British taxi to make my cross-country voyage, I went to the World Wide Web, and voilà. Vintage British taxi found.

I decided I also needed a copilot. It's important to travel alone sometimes, but I was spending enough time in isolation, toiling away at the office by myself, hiding from a relationship that was beginning to crumble. No, I needed a partner in crime for this one, and I knew exactly who to call. Zorba the Greek . . . or the next best thing: my best friend, Steve. Since we had first met a few years before in London, Steve's film career had also brought him to Los Angeles, where we were now not only friends, but frequently creative partners. Steve had been the one friend who continued to motivate me even when I wasn't sure what I was doing. He believed so clearly in my potential and in my dreams, that even when I didn't have faith in myself, I could always borrow the faith that Steve had in me.

But it wasn't long before my adventurous companion began to sound more like the buttoned-down Basil. "Do you know how to fix cars?" Steve asked.

"No," I replied, not really thinking that was a requisite of my plan.

"Did you get someone to check the car before you bought it?" Steve continued.

"Not really." My confidence was beginning to falter a little.

"Not really?"

"Sort of, but not properly," I responded. I had taken the cab to a mechanic I had found in the phonebook and who claimed he worked on vintage cars. I found out, though, that he meant more like 1998 Honda vintage, not a twenty-five year-old London taxi.

"Do you have any clue what you're doing?" Steve asked.

"Absolutely not!" I cried.

But that was the point. I needed to do something about which I had absolutely no clue. I needed to get that taxi, hit the road, and let go of everything I thought was about to happen. I had discovered long ago that nothing frees us like the open space of an empty road: music blasting, windows down, the great world begging us into its embrace and away from the computer screens that pull us at every turn. I needed to disconnect from the Web and reconnect with the world. I needed to dance.

We live in a world that is often lined up for us perfectly. We go to school. We go to college. We get a job. We have a family. We live out our days according to some prearranged plan. But who says that plan needs to be followed? The media? Our family? Our friends? Mark Zuckerberg?

Too many of us hold on so tightly to the preconceived idea of what life is supposed to be like that we fail to let life live us. We try so hard to direct our circumstances that we forget that the world itself might be a much better director. Some people call that force God. Others just view it as the current that runs underneath us at all times,

The world has its own rhythm.

guiding us through life. We can either swim against it, or we can jump into the water and let go, enjoying the ride even as we question its twists and turns.

It was time for me to jump into the raging rapids. And I was calling this ride the Kindness Cab. Because it wasn't going to be a typical road trip. Steve and I were going to be giving people free rides along the way. Picking people up at bus stops, offering them a way home, rescuing them from the side of highways with their thumbs extended. The chorus to my new life song would go something like this: "The Kindness Cab is coming! The Kindness Cab is coming! Free cab rides for all! Kindness is coming to town."

Of course when I sang the song to Steve, he began to re-think his decision to join me on this adventure.

"Are you feeling okay, Leon?" he asked.

"Steve, do you ever feel like if you send one more e-mail, you'll lose your mind?"

"Sometimes," he replied.

"Well, we're not sending any e-mails. We're going to go out and meet people face-to-face instead. We are going to *be* the Internet!"

I could hear him sigh lightly before offering his tentative promise, "I'll try to keep you out of trouble, at least."

"Trouble is what we're looking for," I replied. It was time to find some trouble. But the good kind. The type of trouble we learn from. The type of trouble that teaches us not to fear trouble so much. The type of trouble that demands, like Zorba, that we cut the strings to those routines and responsibilities and digital demands, so we can finally live.

GETTING STARTED

We began at Times Square, from which we planned to travel across America in our vintage London cab, ultimately winding our way to the Hollywood sign. I'd done this before. But the last time, I was getting rides from others. This time, I would be offering the rides. My 1986 London Sterling cab, like all cabs from that era, had pillows, carpets, flowers, and lots of room to chat. During each trip, the meter would be running, but instead of charging the people we picked up, we donated our own money, equaling what their fare would have been, to charity.

The cab had been shipped from Santa Fe, New Mexico, to New York City. When I arrived in New York and saw it in person for the first time, I knew I was screwed. The car was only twenty-five years old, but it looked (and behaved) far more antiquated than that. And when I started the engine, I knew not only that I was screwed, but also that I was never making it to Los Angeles. Ever.

I called Steve, who was getting ready to meet me in New York, and said, "It's over."

"What's over?" Steve asked, still remembering our last conversation, in which I was singing the Kindness Cab jingle.

"The journey. This cab can't make it across America. It's impossible."

"Ye of little faith," he replied.

"You haven't seen the bloody cab, Steve!" I complained. "It hardly even works! We are finished."

"What happened to letting go? What happened to getting into trouble?"

He had a point, but he hadn't seen the cab. We agreed that Steve would be the one to decide whether the Kindness Junker could make it across America. I realized that if I wanted to dance, it might make more sense for someone else to take the lead on this one.

Steve arrived the next day. Having grown up tinkering with motorcycles and old cars, Steve was much more of an expert than I was. After looking over the cab, Steve decided there was about two days of work that needed to be done in order for us to safely start our adventure.

> Real change doesn't happen at the conscious level.

"I'm not sure she'll make it all across the states," he warned. "But at least we'll get started."

And that's the first step toward letting go. Sometimes you just have to at least get started. Sometimes you just have to take that first step even if you're not quite sure where you're going or how you're going to get there.

Because here is another side effect of the Internet. It makes us incredibly independent. Some of you might remember the days before Google Maps. We used to have to get directions from real, live people (and the occasional printed map). They would tell us take a left, then a right. They might even offer us their home phone number in case we got lost. If we wanted to find a great restaurant, we asked someone for a recommendation. We started a conversation, and sometimes that conversation led to more. Asking where the best pizza in town was would bring two people together who had never met before. It might have led to a lifelong friendship. Or it might have led to one of those brilliant and fleeting moments of connection that we don't even realize have touched us until we walk away, knowing we have met another kindred spirit along the Way of the Traveler.

But we stop ourselves from having those moments when we're too busy rushing off to the great pizza joint we found on Yelp, determining the best way to get there from Waze, while alternately posting a picture on Instagram and laughing about some celebrity's tweet. We move through life, connected to the Holy Grail with an Apple on its back. And we miss the recommendations of the people around us, because we're too busy Googling for advice. It's not about choosing one over the other. It's about knowing that we can choose both.

Sometimes, we have to allow other people to play the Zorba to our Basil. We need to connect with the people around us who believe in the wild dream even before we do, even if they're a little crazy.

Be all in.

135

When Steve Wozniak developed the first computer system under the name Apple I, he never intended that it would be sold as a fully assembled, printed circuit board (don't ask me what that means). In fact, Steve Jobs did little on the project except to convince Wozniak that they could sell it as such. Jobs explained to Wozniak that even if they weren't successful, they could at least say to their grandkids they had owned their own company. And that is how Apple came to be. Without Steve Jobs's Zorba, Steve Wozniak would have never helped to create the company that has forever altered our world. I guess Steve is a pretty powerful name.

Who's Your Zorba?

We all have Zorbas around us. That doesn't necessarily mean they need to be crazy Greek villagers who like to dance. Rather, Zorbas are simply the people who believe in us even when we can't. Too often, we push back against those who love us most. Our parents or spouses, our friends who refuse to cosign our bullshit. They remind us that we are capable of living our dreams, of embracing the madness a little, of becoming ourselves. So who is your Zorba? Who is willing to point out, even when you fail, that at least you tried? Write down their name, and how can you begin to listen to them more often and more carefully?

_____

_____

_____

_____

_____

_____

_____

THE PLAN
(OR ENTIRE LACK THEREOF)

Before we hit the road, we set everything up. I had a smart phone, which was dubbed the Kindness Cab Hotline. People could call me, tweet me, or send me a message on Facebook, and I would go to their location and pick them up. For this journey, I had money, so accommodations and food weren't an issue. The only issue was the cab. But I had let go . . . so it wasn't, presumably.

We drove the cab, emblazoned with our Kindness Cab logo and the slogan "Free Rides for All," to Columbus Circle, in the heart of New York City, and waited. It didn't take long for people to start asking us about our vintage taxi.

It took a few prospects before our first patron emerged. Jorge was a college student from the South Bronx who was in his first year at Hunter College. As we drove him to class, he explained that he was the first person in his family to go to college.

"Your parents must be proud," Steve replied.

"My parents don't understand," Jorge explained. "They think I am trying to leave them. They think I'll get my degree and never look back."

I adjusted the rearview mirror to see him better.

"I know," I replied. "My family decided what they wanted me to be way before I even knew what I wanted to be."

"Yeah," Jorge scoffed. "My family definitely had their plans for me."

"And what was that?" asked Steve.

> When you get in touch with pain, you are bound to meet hope.

"We have a restaurant. I mean, I'm proud of my parents for building what they did, but their dreams aren't necessarily my dreams."

Jorge looked back out the window.

"Yeah, for a long time I tried to make my family happy, too," I explained. "But I was miserable."

"My family makes me miserable," Jorge admitted.

"Maybe for now, Jorge," I offered, telling him about my own family, about leaving London, about my own father's charge that I was being ridiculous.

And then I told him what I had found along the Way of the Traveler: "Once you start being yourself, you'll be happy wherever you go."

Jorge looked at both Steve and me and said, "So, is this like a therapy cab?"

I laughed, "You're our first passenger, so we're not really sure what kind of cab it is."

Steve interrupted, "It's the Kindness Cab."

"That's right," I remembered, beginning to hum my jingle, but Steve shot me a look.

Steve turned around to Jorge, "We're spreading kindness."

Jorge shrugged his shoulders as we pulled up to his school, "That's cool."

He got out of the car but popped his head back in, "And thanks for the advice."

We watched as he walked into his school. Jorge. Only a few miles from home and yet light-years away from where people expected him to be. For a long time, I thought if I just moved to a new city, got a new girlfriend, became someone else, I would be happy. But really, it wasn't until I removed all those layers of other people, until I was willing to let go of other people's expectations, that I could not only be myself, but also be comfortable wherever I went—whether it was the open roads of America or my family home back in London.

Living in your story can be deadly.

So many of us are raised with similar expectations. Some grow up with the goal of banker or lawyer placed in front of them, others with the goal of running the family business. Some are told to marry a certain type of person, look a certain way. Others are told that they're not going to amount to anything at all, that they're worthless. These stories are just that . . . stories. They don't have to be our truths. The beauty of becoming yourself is that you get to decide your own truth and whether or not those expectations fit into the reality you choose to create.

Which Stories Should You Question?

It's time to reflect on the stories you were told as a child—and perhaps even as an adult. What expectations were put upon you? Think back through those belief systems you were raised with. What values were considered most important? What type of life were you expected to lead? Write three of these expectations down:

1. _____

_____

_____

_____

_____

_____

2. _____

_____

_____

_____

_____

_____

3. _____

_____

_____

_____

_____

Now, read through your three stories, circling the ones you are still living with today. Are you still working in a job that was chosen for you or that you felt pressured to take? That doesn't mean it's necessarily the wrong job. You may have taken over your mother's company and love every minute of it. Sometimes the guidance we receive from others gently pushes us where we need to go. But that doesn't mean we shouldn't ever question guidance. As much as each of us is connected to one another, we are also individuals with our own rights and needs and dreams. We get to determine which guidance we want to follow, and which we need to reject.

After you have circled the stories that still affect your life today, put an X through the ones you want to change. Think about how each one no longer suits you. And then turn your thoughts to your new life story. Think about the life you want to create, freeing yourself entirely of old expectations.

HITTING BUMPS IN THE ROAD

After an amazing adventure in New York—offering rides to everyone from stockbrokers to schoolteachers—we decided to head south to America's capital, Washington, DC. Despite my initial fears, the Kindness Cab was cruising smoothly. Steve and I were relishing our new roles as cabbies. Steve even sang the Kindness Cab jingle with me once or twice. Though I promised him I wouldn't tell anyone that. . . .

After DC, we decided to head west. As we made our way through the rainy streets of the District of Columbia toward Virginia, Steve told me that when I first shared my idea with him, he was dead set against joining me.

Create laughter.

"You were scared," I told him with complete certainty, because you know, I know everything.

"I wasn't scared," Steve jeered. "I just didn't want to help you escape again."

That stung. "I'm not escaping . . ." I began before trailing off, the heavy DC rain falling around us.

"Come on, Leon," Steve continued. "Every time things get

boring, every time you get tired of work, or her, you decide to do one of these crazy adventures. And they're fun—I get it. They can also be mind-numbingly exhausting. I just wasn't sure if I wanted to be hijacked by your need to run."

Remember what I said about yes-men. Well, Steve clearly wasn't one of them.

I decided that the best thing to say was nothing at all. I would give Steve the silent treatment and then he would see how mature I was. But then it was time to get gas.

I pulled into a station, and Steve went in to get provisions. Have you ever eaten sixteen Slim Jims a day for thirty days? No? Good. No one should.

While filling the tank, I was still thinking about Steve's comment, which was pulling at me from all directions. I wasn't running. Or was I?

There is a Greek myth about a virgin huntress named Atalanta, who had no desire for marriage or family. She lived running from one adventure to the next. When her father decided she must marry, she told him that she would do so only with the suitor who could outrun her. So her father held a great footrace. The man who could best her would be her husband. The others would die. Sounds like a great time, huh? Suitor after suitor failed and fell that day, but then a young man by the name of Hippomenes had a brilliant idea. Every time Atalanta got ahead of him, he would roll a golden apple, gifted to him by the goddess Aphrodite, in front of the huntress. Unable to resist the temptation of the apple, she would slow down, ultimately allowing Hippomenes to beat her at the race and become her husband.

Many of us run so fast that we fail to appreciate the magic around us. It takes a special person to know how to catch our attention, how to roll the golden apples right at our feet, so we stop and think about what we are doing. So we are able to stop running and learn how to commit to the adventure around us—whether that adventure is a life on the road, or creating a happy home with the person you love.

When Can You Stop and See the Magic?

We often find ourselves disconnected from the things and people we value most—not because we don't love them, but because we are moving too fast to truly honor them. Where do you need to slow down today? Is it spending more time with your kids or family? Is it watching the sunrise in the morning or the sunset at night? What activities can you begin doing that will reconnect you to the magic in your life?

_____

_____

_____

_____

_____

———————————————————————————

———————————————————————————

———————————————————————————

Steve had rolled a golden apple at my feet, and it made me question my own motives on this adventure. Was this whole trip just another way for me to escape the things I didn't like about my life? Or was it about embracing the things I loved? I was planning to return to my job when the trip was over. I wasn't entirely sure about the fate of my relationship, but I certainly wasn't the only person in the world with "It's complicated" as my chronic relationship status. I just needed this experience to remind me again who I was. Leon, the adventurer. Leon, the person who loved to meet new people. Leon, the man driving a vintage London taxi across America. Leon the Greek. And I didn't mean that in the sense that my own parents were from Greece. I meant it in the sense that I was willing to embrace the madness. I was willing to dance.

Steve emerged from the gas station just as I was putting the pump nozzle back in its holster. We got into the car silently, Steve handed me my Slim Jim, and we headed back to the highway.

But as I began to accelerate, the Kindness Cab choked.

Steve looked over at me. "What did you do?"

"I didn't do anything," I replied defensively. Still angry at his previous accusations, I added, "I told you this car wouldn't make it."

In fact, it sounded like the Kindness Cab wasn't going to make it another block.

"Pull over," was Steve's curt reply.

He got out and looked under the hood. He returned, clearly confused.

"What gas did you put in the car?"

I shrugged, "I don't know."

"What do you mean, you don't know."

"It said ethanol, you know, regular gas."

Steve's hand hit his forehead.

"What?" I asked, getting annoyed again. Really, did he have to be so condescending?

"Ethanol is not regular gas, Leon."

Ethanol would have worked if I had a Prius, but a 1986 London taxi does not run on ethanol gas. It runs on hardy fuel. I hadn't realized there was any difference between the ethanol and the regular gas with which I had previously fueled the vehicle. In the process, I had destroyed my cab—and my journey.

Steve sighed.

"It's okay, Leon," he tried to offer some compassion. "I have an idea."

We choked our way to the closest mechanic, who drained the engine of all the ethanol gas. And then he filled it up with real gas. After that, the cab still wasn't running quite right, but it was good enough.

As we drove through the night, I realized that if I could let go of my ego, fears, and embarrassment in the toughest of moments—moments like Steve and I were having on the road—I would be able to create the deepest connections. Just as diamonds are forged in fire, often friendship is forged in conflict.

Though I had long been accused of running, I was learning to slow down long enough to see the magic along my path. My journey with the Kindness Cab was about meeting new people; it was about showing the world that people were still willing to do something kind, for free. But most importantly, I was trying to live for adventure. And maybe the person who was really learning that lesson was Steve. I had always thought of Steve as my Zorba, but maybe we could both play that role. Because we all have the ability to be Zorba, but we can all also allow fear or uncertainty to turn us back into Basil just as easily.

Experience the total pain of now.

Finally, I broke the silence: "You're not the first person to accuse me of running."

"Leon—" Steve tried to interrupt.

"No, wait," I explained. "I need to say this for me, too. But the truth is, we all have to find what we love in life whether other people understand it or not. Some people like skydiving, and when they're falling through space, I imagine they experience that same sense of freedom that I get when on the road."

"Leon—" he tried again, but I wouldn't let him.

"We all have this one thing, Steve. This one dream, or hobby, or story that when we're doing it, when we're living it, it makes us feel like the people we were meant to be, not the people we've been told we are."

"I know," Steve replied.

"What?" I asked.

"I know. I realized after I said it, Leon, that this is your thing. It's like that kid, Jorge and school. Or me and film. This is what you love. And sometimes it's messy. But you know what? Everything's messy. And I guess it's like you said: We're supposed to be out looking for trouble. We're supposed to be breaking down on the side of the road."

"Well, I don't know about that," I quickly remembered my embarrassment from earlier.

"No, Leon," Steve continued. "Dreams are troublesome. Everyone would pursue them if they weren't. Maybe that's the point: We need to accept trouble not as the exception, but as the norm."

That night I heard Steve in a way that I wasn't able to hear him before. He had rolled the golden apples in my path and forced me to stop long enough to see the magic on our journey. Part of embracing the madness is accepting that trouble is part of that magic; it's what leads us deeper into the mystery of life. And though it might scare or embarrass us while it's happening, it's also where the big lessons take place. Like Steve had said before the trip, we were

> You can't fight reality. It always wins.

certainly going to break down. And we did. We all are going to break down at one point or another. We are going to screw up. We are going to run so fast and so hard, that we miss the big lessons lying right in front of us . . . and sometimes, we are going to overlook the magic, too. But once we accept all that, we no longer have to fear it. We can embrace the madness, and the trouble, and the disaster, and the golden apples quietly littering our path.

How Can You Turn Failure into Success?

Some of my life's biggest failures—or rather, perceived failures—have led to some of my greatest successes. I have had jobs that I didn't want to take lead me to the most fulfilling opportunities, or relationships end, leading me to the biggest realizations. Sometimes the universe closes a door only to open a window. We have all had these turns of fortune, believing that we have failed, when really that failure was only pushing us onto the path that would ultimately take us where we wanted to go. Name three of your "failures" that turned into successes:

1. _____

_____

_____

_____

_____

2. _____

_____

_____

_____

_____

_____

3. _____

_____

_____

_____

_____

Sometimes, it's in making a mess of things that we get to be most free. Like a child playing with finger paints, we finally get to express our truest selves. Splattered in color, drenched in paint, we look in the mirror, and realize that the biggest miracles come from the mess.

AND LAST BUT NOT LEAST, DANCE

We continued our tour across America, picking up tourists on vacation and grandmothers from nursing homes. We gave rides to off-duty police officers, and young people hitchhiking. We were crossing the country, spreading kindness, creating friendships with strangers, and in a lot of cases, giving rides to people who really needed them—single mothers with bags of groceries, older people waiting at the bus stop, even a young man in a wheelchair, making his way across town.

But the real magic of the Kindness Cab was that it made people smile. I saw it every day—in the people we picked up and in the pedestrians on the street. I saw it when I looked in the mirror and caught a glimpse of myself. There was something wonderful about giving something for nothing. On most of my previous adventures, I had been asking others for help, but this time, I was returning the favor.

We tend to match the emotions of those around us. Like water seeking its own level, moods—good or bad—can shift the energy around us, lifting or sinking the spirits of our fellow travelers. Which is why, when in doubt, find the humor. Connect back into the childish side of yourself, or the cheeky side—whichever fits your personality.

Humor defuses because it connects us in ways that few other gestures can. When people ask how I can approach strangers in any country, I tell them it's simple: be funny. I have found that humor is universal, connecting us despite cultural and language differences, uniting us in our ability to laugh.

How Can You Have More Fun?

Unfortunately, so many of us are focused on our routines and responsibilities that we forget how important it is to also take the time to have fun. Remember when you were a kid and would turn your living room into a gigantic fort? Or when climbing a tree was a near daily occurrence? We can still connect back into the laughter of our childhood lives. Even though my own childhood was populated with bullies, it was also filled with the silly fun of summer days and afternoons in the park. We can all re-create those best and most innocent times.

What can you do that is surprising and silly and fun today? Maybe it's as simple as putting on a song and dancing like a lunatic throughout your house. Maybe there's somewhere you can go to celebrate that silliness, perhaps to your local theme park or even an arcade? How can you have fun today? And who can you ask to join you?

_____

_____

_____

_____

_____

_____

We can all be Zorba and we can all be Basil. But being one without the other doesn't make for a very successful life, and without the Zorba, we forget the great joy of being silly.

DANCE, DANCE, ALWAYS DANCE

Steve and I were laughing our way across the United States: Indianapolis, Chicago, Kansas City, Denver. The windows were down, and the music was blasting. The meaningful conversations—like the one we had had with Jorge in New York City—seemed only to deepen along the way. We would politely request that passengers put down their phones, so that real connections could be made. We talked about family, and our fears. I shared my adventures and the wisdom that comes along the Way of the Traveler—learned from all the accidental teachers I had met during my journeys. In turn, I was becoming an accidental teacher of my own. Instead of being the fearful Basil, who turned embarrassment into conflict, I was becoming a freewheeling Zorba, who knew that by letting go, I was making room for greater love.

Outside Denver, we encountered some wintry weather. Our goal had been to make it to LA by early October, but we had simply had too much fun and gotten a bit behind, finding ourselves driving through the Rockies in late October instead. Oh, the difference two weeks can make! Just as the snow began, we saw someone standing on the side of the road, arm outstretched. I looked over at Steve as I began to slow down the vehicle.

"Okay," he agreed, as we came to a stop.

Though Darren was young, he had the slumped shoulders and tangled hair of someone who had lived too long on the road. As he later explained, he had lived on the kindness of strangers for years, sleeping on the couches of friends, camping across America, and unfortunately, spending far too many nights sleeping on the streets.

Darren gratefully buckled himself into the back of the cab, shaking off the light layer of snow that covered him.

"Thank you both so much," he greeted us, suddenly looking around the taxi, and realizing for the first time this was not a typical car.

"What is this?" he asked, a little warily.

"It's the Kindness Cab!" I called out, beginning the first line of my jingle.

"You're doing *what*?" Darren asked.

"We are driving across the states," Steve explained. "Giving free rides to people."

"Wow," Darren was impressed. "How long you been doing that?"

"Almost a month now." Steve was apparently the designated information desk. "We're on our way to California," he continued. "Should be landing there in the next few days."

"Wow," Darren said again before asking, "Why?"

Since Steve was fielding the questions, I figured I would let him take that one, too.

"Because we want to live," was his rather vague, and slightly creepy, reply.

"I think what my friend means is—" I started to explain.

"No, I get it," Darren interrupted. "I mean, I've been on the road probably too long at this point, but there's . . . " He thought for a moment before finishing, "There's a real freedom out here."

We all sat in silence for a while, the snow beginning to fall in heavier waves.

"How long have you been in Colorado?" I asked our new passenger.

"Not really sure," he replied, looking out the window. "After a while, time just sort of floats away."

Darren had a sister in Denver, where he had been staying for the last few months. But there had been a disagreement, and he had headed off into the snow. As I glanced at him, lying in the backseat, clearly exhausted by his own life choices, I couldn't help but think that this is what happens when you never go home. Because, while exhilarating adventure can be found out on the road, we also need the stability of home. And Darren had been living too long without one.

"I know I'll end up going back to my sister's," he said with resignation. "Don't really have anywhere else to go. At least until the end of winter."

As Darren spoke, the snow continued getting heavier, and I could almost feel the Kindness Cab bracing itself against the storm.

Suddenly, the windshield wipers stopped working. And then the headlights. And then slowly the car began to die.

"Um, gentlemen," I interrupted the conversation. "I think we have a problem."

At this point, the snow was coming down in such heavy

drifts that I couldn't see in front of us to drive. I pulled over to the side of the road just as the Kindness Cab took its last breath.

The cab was silent.

Finally, I uttered the first word, "So . . ."

Steve was just slowly shaking his head.

Darren asked innocently, "Do you have AAA?"

I looked toward Steve. "Steve's our AAA."

"Lucky me," Steve quipped. We all agreed that the best thing to do was wait. Give the old cab a few minutes and then see how she felt after a little break.

Silence permeated the car. Our previous conversation was suddenly buried like the road around us. And then we began to feel the cold creep in.

I thought to myself, "What would Zorba do?" It didn't take me long to come to the answer.

"Anyone want to dance?" I asked.

They both looked at me like, well, you know what.

I opened the door. "I'll do it alone if I have to."

Steve was Greek (as in actually from Greece) and, after our several *Zorba the Greek* conversations on the road, knew what was coming.

"Oh hell," he replied, joining me in the snow.

We put our arms around each other and began to slowly dance a traditional Greek dance, moving side by side through the snow, kicking our legs up to a tune we could hear only in our heads. And then we saw it. The back passenger door opened up.

"You two are crazy," Darren shook his head as he approached. "So what are we doing here?"

Steve and I taught him the moves, and together the three of us began to dance as I hummed the music from the film. We danced through the snow, moving faster as the tempo sped up, warming us all in the cold.

Ignite a fire in others.

Finally, a large truck with four-wheel drive pulled up. The driver rolled down the window.

"What the hell are you people doing?"

"We're dancing, man," Darren cried. "We're dancing!"

"I can see that!" he yelled to us, clearly worried. "You need some help?"

"Sure," Steve replied, as the man got out and joined our merry band, laughing at the three men dancing on the side of road.

As I moved to open the hood, I turned to Darren: "This is why we don't have AAA."

I had become Zorba, but more importantly, we all have the chance to become Zorba. We all have the ability to get out of the car—or simply put down our cell phones—and dance. We can also invite the people around us to join in. Rather than dancing, this could be about inspiring our coworkers to run a half-marathon. We could motivate our friends to go skydiving. We could ask our partner to slow dance for no reason on a Wednesday night at home. In doing so, we embrace that touch of madness, and we learn to reconnect with those we love, to connect to the strangers around us. We learn again to live.

How Can You Be Zorba?

So, how can you be Zorba today? Think of three people who are too busy being Basil to embrace the madness around them. And then figure out how you are going to get them to join you. Because we all have the desire to dance. Sometimes, we just need someone to invite us to the floor.

1. _____

_____

_____

2. _____

_____

_____

3. _____

_____

_____

Steve and the truck driver were able to get the cab going again. That is the Way of the Traveler. Each bump ultimately has the opportunity to toss us into the path of someone else. And to push us farther along the course of our dreams. But it's not always easy to see those challenges as opportunities. We have a choice. Either we can allow them to stall us on our journey, or we can come together, bonded by the vulnerability of our shared solitude. But not if we're still connected to our old fears, our old ideas, our old conceptions of how things are supposed to be. We can't live with the freedom of Zorba if we refuse to let go of control, to disconnect, from time to time, from the gadgets and routines that hold our lives in check, and hold us back from our dreams.

Ultimately the best way to pursue your dreams is simply to go for it. One small step at a time. Then take the next step, and eventually, you might find yourself dancing.

SIX

THE WAY TO MASTERY IS GETTING OUT OF YOUR OWN WAY

"When I let go of what I am, I become what I might be."

—LAO TZU

During my first trip to Nepal (you know, the one with Aardash and the sunrise and that first deep awakening about the Way of the Traveler), I ended up in a small English-language bookstore in Kathmandu. It was an expat outpost filled with nomadic travelers from around the world. I decided to pick up something for my plane ride home. As I was perusing the shelves, one book leaped out at me. And I mean that literally. I knocked into a table with books, and one of them fell off, landing at my feet: Paolo Coelho's *The Alchemist*.

Coelho's masterpiece tells the magical story of Santiago,

a shepherd child who travels in search of a worldly treasure. His quest ultimately leads him to riches so very different than any he could have ever imagined. But perhaps the biggest gift comes when Santiago learns that *he* is the biggest obstacle to finding his own treasures.

For most of my early life I thought I was fighting the bullies around me. But through the years, and my adventures, I have come to see that the biggest bully in my life is me. It wasn't an overnight realization (few are), but after I had long released the naysayers from my life, or learned to ignore them, I was still allowing in the one naysayer who had always been there: the one inside my head.

But once I began to get out of my own way, once I began to surrender to the world around me, to the flow of life, that world began to carry me. It allowed me to get out of my head, and to start listening to the other people in my life, even the ones I had long failed to hear.

Like Santiago, I had left home seeking my own journey, and what I found was a world filled with accidental teachers. People who could show me things that I had been unable to learn from those who actually knew me best. Sometimes we can hear the whisper of a stranger far more easily than the shouting of a friend. From the Brazilian peasants who invited me into their home for dinner, teaching me the power of love. From the Peruvian kids who played football with me in the street, teaching me the power of joy. From the Thai riverboat driver who gave free rides to families carrying sick children, teaching me the power of compassion. And from the Vietnamese taxi driver who, when he heard I hadn't spoken to my father in months, told me about his relationship with his own father, teaching me the power of forgiveness. From all these people, and thousands more, I learned to be a student of the world.

The only problem was I believed I had to go to the ends of the world in order to learn those lessons.

I thought wisdom came from the outside, that the Way of the Traveler demanded long and exhausting journeys across barren landscapes and through snake-ridden jungles. I thought I had to struggle and suffer in order to find my treasures. But, like Santiago, I was learning that the path to the life we were meant to live is actually much gentler: All we have to do is be willing to stop fighting ourselves and, often, the ones closest to us.

We have to begin to listen to all the teachers in our lives, even the ones we might have spent our lives ignoring. And then we need to begin to listen to ourselves. We need to learn how to quiet the world around us enough to hear that deep and powerful voice within. That's when the treasures that we seek will ultimately be revealed.

THE TALLEST OAK

In *The Outliers*, Malcolm Gladwell examines how people become successful, trying to determine what ultimately shapes a person into a leader who takes advantage of opportunities and transitions from student to master. Gladwell observes: "The tallest oak in the forest is the tallest not just because it grew from the hardiest acorn; it is the tallest also because no other trees blocked its sunlight, the soil around it was deep and rich, no rabbit chewed through its bark as a sapling, and no lumberjack cut it down before it matured."

Growing up, I looked up to my father as the tallest oak. He was a stoic lion, and I was his unruly cub. He loomed large, and not just because of his professional success. He loomed large because he was in charge of his own destiny. Even as a child, I knew that my father was his own boss, and the boss of us all.

Though I came from the hardiest acorn, you could say it took me a bit longer to grow out of my father's shadow.

Like many, I blamed the people who loved me most for my awkward beginnings. I blamed my parents for the bullies at school. When I started to lose myself in too many pints of beer, I blamed them for that, too. I thought that the way I behaved was because of the way I was raised.

For many of us, our most complicated relationship is the one we have with our parents. It makes sense. We have the longest histories with them. They were there from the moment of our first breaths, teaching us the life lessons and belief systems with which they themselves were raised. Unless, of course, they de-

Commit to yourself.

cided to break free from the traditions of their own upbringing. Some of us are fortunate enough to have parents who were either raised with healthy belief systems about the world and themselves, or who surrendered the beliefs they were given and developed a healthy system on their own. But the rest of us come from generations rooted in old ideas about how the world works. Some of us had parents who taught us that we were perfect and blessed just the way we were. Others offered us a more complex view of the world and of ourselves. These belief systems were often rooted in fear and trauma and scarcity, all elements of the worlds our ancestors grew up with. And as we grew, we created our own belief systems, which were often amended versions of what was passed down to us that ultimately influenced our life choices.

And most of us didn't even recognize that we were doing it.

I emulated the tall and hardy tree, and believed that as long as I was financially successful, nothing else mattered. And maybe had I been a different person, that would have been fine. But when I garnered financial success, I thought my misery was merely a lack of gratitude. I didn't understand that I was a different kind of tree.

The Way of the Traveler offers us a different perspective. As we create our own life, we begin to evaluate and reshape the belief system that was instilled in us. We are able to determine what works for our life and dreams, and what doesn't. We begin to accept into our own truths, and not just the ones passed down for generations.

And so our relationship with our parents changes. Sometimes, it's gradual and we don't even notice when it happens, or that it's already happened. Other times, we know the exact moment that we let go of the past.

Three years ago, I was in the middle of crossing the globe, literally. I had just turned thirty-six and was riding a yellow motorcycle across the world, with no money, no food, and no lodging, except for that offered by strangers I met along the way. For anyone who has read my book *The Kindness Diaries*, this will all sound very familiar.

Along this journey, I had been given a very important invitation: to meet with the head of the Eastern Orthodox Church, a man referred to as "the first among equals." Basically, the Pope of the Eastern Orthodox Church.

But what surprised me even more than the invitation was that my father wanted to join me.

Over the years, I had moved across the world, pushing my family further and further away. I thought that I needed to make it on my own—to show them just how tall of an oak I could be—that I didn't need their help to get there.

I pushed them away, and then I acted as though they had abandoned me.

But then I went to Istanbul to meet the "first among equals" with my father, and that illusion of abandonment disappeared.

As I pulled into the ancient town, I was reminded just how exotic the world can be. Because for all of Istanbul's modern buildings and bridges, it is still clear that the city has been around for many millennia. The rising spires of the 1,500-year-old Hagia Sophia church and the red-tiled roofs of the old city are a constant reminder of the past.

My father and I met outside the patriarch's complex, comprised of several small, modern buildings settled around the cathedral of St. George. The patriarch's assistant came out and told us there had been a scheduling conflict. He explained that we could wait if we wanted, but that the patriarch was running late.

I knew my father had another appointment, but he replied to the assistant, "We can wait."

After the assistant left, I murmured, "Well, you came all this way to see him."

My father laughed, "I didn't come here to see him. I came here to see you."

It had never before occurred to me that my father might miss me. All my life I had been telling myself a story that suddenly didn't make sense. I had believed that I was the unloved, unwanted runt of the litter. That my father pitied me, but didn't really love me. I had believed that it didn't matter how I behaved because he didn't care anyway. I had held on so tightly to this story that, even after finding my own voice and my own success, my father was still stuck in a role that I had created for him. But in that moment, the well-crafted illusion that had allowed me to keep him at arm's length began to unravel.

"You're always on the move, Leon," he continued. "You're

not an easy man to pin down. I figured this was one appointment neither of us would miss."

He stopped for a second, and I realized that he was fighting back tears. All my life, I had thought of him as being indestructible. He was that tall, unshakable, unmovable tree. I never realized that I, the wayward acorn, could shake him.

"I miss you," he finally uttered.

Suddenly, it hit me. My father was human. He wasn't a god among men. He was simply the first among equals. And I was his equal. I was his son. And it was time I finally stopped fighting his love for me. It was time I stopped fighting myself.

While I was busy learning from the accidental teachers I met along my journey, I had failed to listen to my own father. I had locked him out of my life, and my life choices. And all he wanted was to be invited along. After all those years of pushing my father away, I felt myself begin to surrender to the truth of our relationship. We were very different people in some ways: My father didn't question his actions, or at least didn't show it. He moved with the type of confidence that I don't know if I will ever have. And I was clearly the more sensitive type, like my mother, whose heart could break over a stranger's story. But for once, I was able to surrender my judgment of both of us. Instead, I began to accept that we were who we were, and

> Presence is power.

that no matter what, we meant an enormous amount to each other.

The assistant came back out to us. "Good news," he declared. "The patriarch can see you now."

Together, my father and I walked into the patriarch's office. The first among equals blessed my father and then turned to me.

The story of my travels had come to his attention. For my blessing, he offered, "Greetings for Leon Logothetis: The first and last letters of the Greek word for love, *agape*, are the first and last letters of the Greek alphabet, alpha and omega. It is our prayer and hope that you will discover this love from one end of the world to the other."

I looked over at my father. He didn't have to say a word for me to know he was proud of who I had become.

After the patriarch's blessing, I offered to give my father a ride back to his hotel. We walked to my yellow motorcycle. For the first time, he saw my trusty steed. It was streaked in mud. It was missing one of its mirrors. There was a sizable dent in the gas tank.

Commit to your greatness.

"Jesus," he exclaimed. "That's what you're driving across the world?"

"I call her Kindness One," I told him. "It's running on the kindness of others."

He looked at me with the same expression he wore nearly

ten years before when I first told him I was quitting my job and traveling around the world.

"Leon, you are something else," he laughed as he climbed into my sidecar.

I stopped for a second. How many moments had I missed in my life because I was too busy worrying about my own fears and resentments to see them? There was my father, his hair now gray, his face and body an older, softer version of the man I grew up with. He looked like a child, smiling in the sidecar. And as I got on the bike, I wanted to hold on to that moment forever.

We rode through the streets of Istanbul, a perfect breeze accompanying us as my father let go, and allowed me to lead the way.

My journeys across the world have allowed me to meet so many different types of people. Everywhere I go, I learn something new, something I can take back with me to everyday life. Perhaps the most important of these lessons involved learning that we must all be willing to let go of who we think we are in order to become ourselves.

I thought about the patriarch's words: "The first and last letters of the Greek word for love, *agape*, are the first and last letters of the Greek alphabet, alpha and omega. It is our prayer and hope that you will discover this love from one end of the world to the other."

Every journey, every relationship is an opportunity to discover that love. To surrender the lies we have built between and about the people around us. That surrender can happen between a thirty-six-year-old son and his father. Or it can happen between two strangers on the street who let go of any prejudices or preconceived ideas they might have about each other. It can happen when, instead of crossing the street to avoid someone, we slow down and smile. It can happen when a rabbi opens the door for an imam.

The Way of the Traveler was showing me that in giving up my old story about being the runt of the lion's litter, I could finally move out from my father's shade. As I continued my travels after Istanbul, I was creating my own destiny, but I would only be able to embrace its treasure if I stopped fighting myself and my old ideas along the way.

Instead of struggling against my own roots, I could find a sunny place in the world in which to grow. That didn't mean I had to leave my father behind. I simply needed to invite him along. I needed to offer him shotgun on the adventure that had become my life. As I saw that day, he gladly accepted my offer.

How Can You Reinvent Your Relationships?

Most of us have been challenged by the relationships we have with our parents, or the people who raised us. And if you're like me, we have often allowed those old stories to define and shape who we are, but that doesn't mean they have to continue to do that. What is your current relationship like with the people who raised you? What are those old stories you tell yourself about that relationship? And how can you begin to write a new story?

_____

_____

_____

_____

_____

_____

THE LESSONS OF LETTING GO

By the time I was twelve, I knew I was a bad student. I didn't even care if I did well or not, because I knew my role. Teachers would look at me with dismay on the first day of class, seemingly disappointed that my name had appeared on their student list. By the time I made it to university, I was no longer interested in "being good." I started skipping class. Staying out too late. Drinking too much. I stopped respecting the people around me, and I stopped respecting myself. I would wake up with a hangover and say, "I'm never going to do that again."

Then the next week, I would be doing it again. By now, we've all heard the definition of insanity: doing the same thing over and over and expecting different results. But a lot of people simply can't stop whatever insane thing they are doing. For some, it's a bad relationship. For others, it's their relationship with food. Shopping, smoking, gambling, lying, money, alcohol, drugs, sex, love—these are all things we can be addicted to, and they can make anyone insane. But another part of addiction is how we react to our feelings. Because whether or not we reach for an outside substance or engage in an unhealthy behavior, we can all become overwhelmed by how we feel, by how we handle fear, misery, depression, self-pity, or failure.

In his autobiography, *The Heroin Diaries*, rocker Nikki Sixx defines addiction as "when you can give up something anytime, as long as it's next Tuesday." Addiction is less about what you're addicted to and more about the relationship you have with that thing. It's about relying on something else to help you cope, to help you work, to help you live, to help you get through the day.

Observe resistance.

And more often than not, it's really about what's hiding underneath. Now, I'm no doctor—far from it—so I will say this: If you think you have an addiction to something, you should seek medical help. Whether that be a doctor, a psychiatrist, or a treatment facility, reach out to someone who can guide and advise you.

That is the one thing you can do today.

Because addiction can kill. But in recognizing and changing the feelings that drive the addiction, we can finally become free. Realizing that we are relying on food or relationships or alcohol or shopping in order to get through life means we probably have a lot to get through. We have a lot of fear. We have a lot of pain. And we think the only way to feel better is to continue dancing with our addiction.

For years, I couldn't let go of that drink. It steadied me in a world that felt off-kilter. It allowed me to be me because I was afraid of the world. But even more painfully, I was afraid of being myself. I needed liquid courage just to feel comfortable in my own skin. It was heartbreaking, and it was horrible, and it took me to more dark corners than I ever imagined I would go.

Then one day, I got tired of waking up, wishing away another night. I looked in the mirror, and I knew that I couldn't keep making the promise that tomorrow I would stop. Because how many more todays was I going to waste before I got to that tomorrow?

In *The Alchemist*, Santiago's journey is delayed when he finds a lucrative job along his travels. He questions whether he should go on or whether the material riches laid before him are the real treasure. For the first time, Santiago is a wealthy man. But he knows that the wealth stands between him and his true self.

> There is no pain like exposed denial.

I knew that drinking, albeit a temporary salve, was standing between the person I was at that time, and the person I hoped to be. I knew, just as Santiago knew, that the universe offered more, if only I were willing to see it.

But I had no clue what that "more" was. I didn't know that once I stopped drinking, the whole world would open up before me. I didn't know that I would feel at one with all the people within it. Or most importantly, that I would feel at one with myself.

Then I met Louise. I was driving through California when I stopped off in a desert town for the night. It was one of those small, dusty places that felt trapped back in a different time, like the Westerns I watched as a kid, leading me to think that the whole of America looked like the set of *Bonanza*. I decided to head to a local bar. At that point, I was already tired of waking up wanting a different life. I just didn't know how to get it.

I sat down at the bar and ordered a beer. Next to me sat a woman who looked like a reincarnated Janis Joplin. Heavy silver rings adorned her fingers, and her suede fringe jacket hung over the edge of the bar stool.

She introduced herself and asked where I was from. We started talking, and I discovered that Louise was originally from Texas, but had moved out to this dusty town years before.

"It feels like Texas probably felt back when my grandmother was young," she explained. "Texas doesn't feel like this anymore."

I ordered another beer as the talk turned to our lives. Louise ran a local motel, and lived up the empty dirt road from the bar where we were sitting.

"It's fun," she explained. "I used to love to travel, but now the travel comes to me. I get to see the whole world pass through my doors. The whole world and all its problems."

As I went for another beer, I noticed Louise was still drinking hers. I offered to buy her one, and she told me she didn't drink.

"This here's root beer," she explained. "I quit the good stuff years ago."

Louise explained that she had grown tired of living life through booze-colored glasses. "Everything just seemed so hazy," she explained. "I remembered when I was a kid, the world being this clear, brilliant place filled with possibility, and then suddenly it just felt like the world kept getting smaller and smaller and darker and darker."

"So what did you do?" I asked her.

"Have you ever heard the story of the two wolves?" she asked me.

"I have," I told her, knowing that there were two wolves, the wolf of light and the wolf of darkness.

"No," she stopped me as I began telling her the story. "The wolves are not light and dark. The wolves are joy and sorrow. And you get to decide, which wolf do you want to feed?"

I realized that through drinking, I had only been fueling my sorrow. As Louise continued, I understood that it had been the same for her, too. She shared with me, "I realized that it wasn't just the booze. It was about all the choices I was making in my life. I decided it was time to quit drinking. But most important, it was time I quit lying to myself. I wanted to see the world again."

All those stories about who we are and what we need in order to be okay feed one of two wolves, that of sorrow or that of joy. We get to decide which we want to feed. Do we want to make choices that will lead to joy? Or do we want to consistently find ourselves back in sorrow, believing that another slice of cake, another trip to the mall, or another drink at the bar will make it all go away? As I walked out of the bar that night, I knew what choice I wanted to make.

Quitting drinking wasn't easy work, and it wasn't a simple decision. It was hard and painful and awkward and completely humbling. Still, today, many years later, I can remember those first few months of painful rediscovery, of getting to know myself once again, and maybe for the first time. But it's like the old saying, "When you're going through hell, keep going." I knew I had to keep going. I knew that if I truly wanted to be my best self, I had to be free from everything that held me back. Everything.

I never saw Louise again. I didn't have to. Sometimes accidental teachers show up for just a moment to help us loosen our grip on the things we think we need. They show us instead where we need to surrender. Where we continue to stand in our own way between the lives we are leading and the ones we were meant to live.

What is all this costing you?

177

How Can You Change Your Behavior?

Though we might bristle at the term, most of us are addicted to something. We're addicted to being busy. We're addicted to complaining. We're addicted to waking up every morning and thinking about how our lives can be different, which is why so many of us are addicted to Facebook, Twitter, or Instagram. We are addicted to envying the lives of others, and failing to see the beauty of our own. If there is something right now that is standing between you and your potential, ask yourself, am I addicted to that thing? And what can I do today to change that?

Go ahead, start here. Write down three things that stand in your way of creating or appreciating the beautiful life that stands before you:

1. _____

_____

_____

_____

_____

2. _____

_____

_____

_____

_____

3. _____

_____

_____

_____

_____

When I first started meditating, I couldn't stop thinking. I wanted to plan my day. I wanted to make that to-do list and check it twice. All my life, I had thought that joy was an action. If only I did something, I would produce joy as a result.

But joy is not an action. It is a state of being. Joy is not breathing; it is breath.

As Coelho writes in *The Alchemist,* "It's the simple things in life that are the most extraordinary; only wise men are able to understand them."

More often than not, we receive that wisdom in the silence of surrender, not in the loud voice of determination. We have to stop doing in order to start being.

Letting go of drinking taught me how to let go of other behaviors. I didn't have to take huge actions. I didn't have to run a marathon to change my life; I just had to take a walk. The Way of the Traveler has taught me that there are always two paths: the challenging one and the easy one. Both are courageous in their own right. Sometimes we need to take the challenging path. Sometimes it offers the better views; it provides the needed lessons. And sometimes, the kinder, gentler path is the way to go. There are times in my life when I need to take the three-day train ride to New York, and there are times when I need to take the five-hour flight. The Way of the Traveler shows us how to remove the branches and debris that cover this gentler way. It helps us remove those addictions and obstacles, those fears and insecurities that stand between us and our ability to connect with the world.

How Can You Surrender to Your Spirit?

In order to find that adventurous road, we have to be able to hear the spirit within. We need to find ways to get quiet enough to hear our inner intuition at work. Too often we ignore this inner voice and find ourselves on the wrong path instead, tiring ourselves out needlessly or failing to go on the adventure our spirit needs most. Think about how you can begin to connect to that spirit. Think of the place where you have been able to hear that part of yourself most clearly and commit to creating a practice around it. Is it meditation or taking a walk every day? How can you take the time to listen to that spirit within?

_____

_____

_____

_____

_____

_____

When we begin to let go of certain behaviors, we discover what is hiding just below: our quiet spirit. We discover our compassion for others and begin to have compassion for ourselves. We all want to love. The only thing that stops that from happening is fear—fear that we won't get what we want, or what we need. Fear that we aren't worthy of such lives. Fear that we don't have it in us to make those lives happen.

But we all have it in us.

When I left that California bar, I realized that I didn't need a drink to connect me to you. The drink was just another bully, telling me I was worthless without it. Once I let go of it, I found out I hadn't even scratched the surface of my worth. Suddenly, all those dreams I had in the barroom became possibilities. Because in order to go out and find the life you want, you first need to learn how to appreciate the one you have.

STEP BACK

Then one morning, at the age of thirty-eight, I ended up alone, wet, and frightened in a jungle in Ecuador. But let's back up for a second.

Do you remember Naasih from India? Well, I decided it was time for me to move from being the student to becoming the teacher. I asked Naasih to train me in coaching other people through their lives, and he agreed. He was going to be leading a group through Ecuador (much as he had led me through India), so I went as his assistant.

"Are you ready for this, Leon?" he asked.

"Of course," I replied, absolutely sure in my intentions, resolute in my determination, unwavering in my . . . well, you get the idea.

And then I landed in Ecuador. Over the next week, I slept three hours, at the most, each night, often on the hard and wet ground in various villages. We were on the move all day, taking a group of six fellow seekers across the country, through jungles, onto the sea, weaving our way through cities and the countryside. And in the process, we were showing them the world without a net.

By the sixth day, I was exhausted. Sleep deprivation is a cruel master. Some days, there wouldn't even be time to eat. I had lost five pounds in as many days. And though we were showing the group the world without a net, I was desperately wishing for one just so I could lie down and go to sleep.

*Take care
of your self.*

Finally, I went to Naasih, and told him I needed a break.

"There are no breaks, Leon," he told me. "If you are not ready for this, you don't need to be here."

"It's just one night," I explained. "I just need one night of sleep."

Naasih didn't say anything at first, but then with his usual candor, he replied, "I don't think you understand why you're doing this."

"But I do," I began to argue, even as I found myself asking the same question. Why was I doing this? What more did I need to find? I *had* seen jungles and villages. I had been sick at sea. Why did I keep coming back for more? Was I seeking enlightenment, or was I just punishing myself in an attempt to attain it?

I was reminded again of *The Alchemist*: "Before a dream is realized, the Soul of the World tests everything that was learned along the way. . . . That's the point at which most people give up. It's the point at which, as we say in the language of the desert, one 'dies of thirst just when the palm trees have appeared on the horizon.'"

I didn't want to die of thirst, but at the same time, I also couldn't see any palm trees on the horizon.

I walked back to the group that night, despondent. I didn't want to give up. I had learned from my father, from some of my better schoolteachers, from the whole of the British Empire, not to mention Winston Churchill himself, that we never, ever, ever give up.

How was I ever going to become a teacher if I couldn't make it as a student?

After the group went to bed, I cleaned up the dinner and camp. It was an earlier night, and I was grateful that I would at least get five hours of sleep.

It seemed like only moments after I had fallen asleep, that someone was shaking me awake. Naasih stood over me.

"Let's go," he whispered.

"Do you never sleep?" I asked as I rose to join him on yet another quest.

"Get your things," was his only reply.

We moved quietly out of the camp and got into one of the Jeeps we used to travel through the surrounding jungles.

"Where are we going?" I wondered out loud, knowing better than to expect a reply.

Together, we drove in silence for an hour through the dark night.

Finally, Naasih stopped the car. I couldn't see where we were, but from the bumpy ride, I knew we were far from civilization.

"Get out," Naasih said.

I didn't move.

"I said, 'Get out,'" he repeated.

"Why?" I asked.

"When you are ready to lead, come back to the camp."

I looked out into the blackness of the night. "You don't have to leave me here in order for me to lead."

"I'm sorry, Leon, but I do."

I sucked in my breath, and got out of the car.

I watched as the lights of Naasih's car faded in the distance. And then I realized. I was in the bloody jungle. It was the middle of the night. I didn't know where I was. I didn't know what to do. And I hate bloody jungles.

And then it began to rain.

There I stood in the Ecuadorian jungle, the rain coming

down around me. I didn't know where I was. I didn't know where I was going. I knew that I could follow the road that would presumably lead me back to camp, but is that where I wanted to go?

Douglas Tompkins, noted adventurer and cofounder of The North Face, once said, "What happens when you get to the cliff? Do you take a step forward or do you make a 180-degree turn and take one step forward? Which way are you going? Which is progress?"

feeling safe is a form of control.

I was standing on the edge of that cliff. But what was pushing me there? Was I being motivated by love? Or was I being motivated by fear? I thought about his words: "When you are ready to lead, come back to the camp."

But maybe I didn't want to be the type of leader that always went back to the camp. Maybe going forward wasn't progress. Maybe progress was making that 180-degree turn.

Too often in life, we allow the people around us to make our decisions for us. We are guided by our parents, spouses, friends, or teachers and not by the dictates of our own souls. Often, we call that surrender, but really, we are fighting against our own inner truths. It's no wonder we end up anxious or depressed. We are at odds with the great powerful wave within ourselves, swimming against the tide of our rightful destiny.

I sat down on that wet jungle floor and let the rain drench me. There was nothing more for me to do. I had walked to the edge of the cliff one last time. And I knew it was time to go home.

I remembered that when I first read *The Alchemist*, I thought the book was about going out into the world to find one's gold. Sitting on that cold, muddy floor, I realized it's really about going out into the world in order to discover that the treasure you seek is waiting for you at home. The treasure has been inside you this whole time. That is the great secret.

The Way of the Traveler shows us that sometimes the destination is actually the starting point. Alpha and omega. It's not about the people who raised us. It's not about the things we use or the things we do that we think are making us happy. It's not about the great big adventures into the world. It's about ourselves. It's about that quiet place inside where the Way of the Traveler truly resides. It is that great big adventure within that teaches us the biggest lessons.

At the end of *The Alchemist*, Santiago finally returns home, only to discover that buried underneath the tree in his backyard is the treasure he was seeking this whole time. As I sat in that jungle, the night just beginning to turn into day, I realized that there was a huge adventure waiting for me. And it didn't include any new stamps in my passport.

Can You Find the Treasure Within?

Too often we're so consumed with what we need to change, that we fail to see what is already working, what is already wonderful. We spend so much time examining our flaws that we forget what incredible qualities we hold inside. So, what are your treasures—the qualities that draw people to you, the reasons your friends love you? Is it your sense of humor or your sense of loyalty? Is it your creativity or your kindness? List five of them here:

1. _____

_____

2. _____

_____

3. _____

_____

4. _____

_____

5. _____

_____

As the sun rose in the Ecuadorian jungle that morning, I stood up, wet, exhausted, and more alive than I had ever been. I made my way to the main road, and hitchhiked back into the nearest town. I wasn't going back to camp. I didn't need to. It was time I got out of my own way. It was time I stopped believing that I needed to struggle in order to learn. It was time I embraced the gentler path.

We all have that choice. We can keep holding onto those old stories and behaviors and relationships, or we can begin to surrender them all and find just beneath a deep and powerful spirit waiting to rise up within us all.

Go wander.

Santiago's journey in *The Alchemist* leads him across the world and into the desert of his own spirit, but ultimately, the journey is about what he does with those teachings when he returns home. I knew that it was time for me to go home. It was time for me to take the teachings of the Way of the Traveler and find a way to share them with others.

SEVEN

GIVING BACK
IS THE ONLY WAY
TO TAKE IN LIFE

"What is the use of living, if it be not to strive for noble causes and to make this muddled world a better place for those who will live in it after we are gone?"

—WINSTON S. CHURCHILL

I got Winston when he was twelve weeks old. He was a tiny Boston Terrier, and was the smallest, most fragile thing I had ever held in my hands. And I knew, much like I imagine new parents realize to a far larger degree, that I was entirely responsible for the health and well-being of this new pup's life.

I loved him instantly. In fact, I loved him like I had never loved anything or anyone else before. Over the years, I watched as Winston grew from that tiny little twelve-week-old runt into a gentle, opinionated, and very funny dog. And yes, dogs very much have senses of humor. Have you never seen YouTube?

And through the years, Winston watched me grow. He witnessed my breakups and heartbreaks; he waited patiently for me as I traveled the world and changed professions; and he curled up next to me on mornings when I felt like I had no one else in the world. But I always had Winston.

As Rudyard Kipling wrote in *Just So Stories*, "When the Man waked up he said, 'What is Wild Dog doing here?' And the Woman said, 'His name is not Wild Dog any more, but the First Friend, because he will be our friend for always and always and always.'"

Winston was my First Friend. And he was mine for always and always and always.

More than any person I have ever known, Winston taught me one of life's most powerful lessons—he showed me how to love unconditionally. After a while, I began to realize that if I treated everyone in my life the way I treated Winnie, as I called him, I would be a much happier man, and so would the people around me. I began to call it Winnie Love.

Winnie Love asks that we treat everyone with the same forgiveness and tenderness that we would treat our favorite pet. Whether it's directed at our parents or a homeless person on the street, Winnie Love shows us that compassion shouldn't be limited to our four-legged friends; compassion should be the breath of our lives.

Not long ago, I was having a cup of coffee at Starbucks.

Winston was with me, and as usual, he was quick to introduce me to the world.

The guy sitting next to us couldn't help but stop to play with Winnie, and we began to talk about our love of dogs.

Shine light and love onto yourself and others.

My fellow dog lover was named Bertrand, and he practiced what he called, "awesome acts of Good Samaritan-ism." He had made quite a bit of money in the stock market, invested it in ways to always "keep me rich," and decided to spend his days doling out surprise gifts to people he met along the way.

So I told him about Winnie Love.

He clapped his hands in appreciation. Then I explained to him where in my life I was lacking in my own Winnie Love. I'm sure you're thinking, "Geez, Leon, you just met the guy." But that is part of the definition of Winnie Love. It is learning to be so vulnerable with a stranger that you can find yourself in the deepest of conversations within minutes simply by admitting to a broken heart.

At that point, my girlfriend Lina and I had been together a few years. I had just come back from my six-month tour around the world by motorcycle. I had crossed four continents and three oceans with no money, and in turn, I had given life-changing gifts to some of the people I met along the way. I had helped a homeless man in Pittsburgh get an apartment and return to school. I had helped a rickshaw driver in India buy his own business. I had helped a single mother with HIV build a home for her and her son in Cambodia.

"But," I explained to Bertrand, "I can't seem to give in my own relationships."

In fact, Lina and I were breaking up. I bent down and patted Winston's head, feeling my blood pressure drop just by touching his fur. I often call dogs canine Prozac, because they are the universe's most natural antidepressant. And just then, I was battling depression, as I have many times in my life. The type of depression that sends you to doctors, the kind of depression that is determined to keep you in bed.

The truth is, relationships are hard for everyone. But somehow, I felt that I was particularly bad at them. It was the one area in which I was failing to apply all the amazing lessons I had learned along the Way of the Traveler. I was failing at my own teachings. And there is nothing like failure to make you feel like you don't have much to offer the world. I was retreating again to the safety of my bed and my gallon of ice cream. And I knew it was all because I wasn't being my best person to the one I loved most.

Bertrand nodded knowingly.

"Giving is different for everyone," he explained. "For some people, it is very easy for them to give to their mothers or husbands or children. But they would never even think of donating to a stranger, and for some of us, it's the opposite. Either way, giving is all about practice. The more we give, the more comfortable we become with giving, so that one day we can give to everyone in equal measure."

PRACTICE, PRACTICE, PRACTICE

I don't know the point in my life when I realized giving to others was basically the biggest thrill in the world. I grew up in a family that always believed in being generous to people who had less than we did. We donated money and collected canned goods and used clothes, but it wasn't until much later that I discovered what it means to truly give to someone else. The Way of the Traveler shows us we won't get very far on our own. We have to share the path with others, and just as they give to us along the journey, so we give to them. Even if it means opening up your heart to a stranger and seeing for a moment what it might be like to walk their road, and maybe just for a day or even a minute, choosing to walk alongside them.

As Daniel Goleman writes in *Social Intelligence*, "Self-absorption in all its forms kills empathy, let alone compassion. When we focus on ourselves, our world contracts as our problems and preoccupations loom large. But when we focus on others, our world expands. Our own problems drift to the periphery of the mind and so seem smaller, and we increase our capacity for connection—or compassionate action."

I was able to have compassion for strangers, but then why did I fail when the connection hit closer to home? As I realized in that coffee shop, despite dedicating my life to finding the vagaries of human connection, when I am put in a situation with someone close to me, I fumble. I flail. I flounder. Why? Simple: I am scared.

I often think back to that childhood gaffe, when I handed the sweet little China plate to my crush, and she handed it back to me with my heart upon it. In many ways, I had gone on to give people I met on the street those intimate gifts of kindness, but when I thought someone could really break my heart, I had kept the China cabinet locked. But maybe Bertrand was right; maybe it was all about practice.

Most of us struggle with the act of giving because it's natural to be self-absorbed. It's also normal to be scared. Some of us show up for our loved ones, but ignore the needs of the stranger on the street. Others, like yours truly, find it easier to be of service to strangers than to the ones we love most.

Because when we truly connect to another person, we become vulnerable. And it's easier to hide behind our walls of self-absorption than to risk our hearts by reaching out. How often have we seen an opportunity to help a stranger? Maybe it's as clichéd as helping an elderly man cross the road, or offering to help put a woman's groceries in her car as she struggles with two screaming toddlers and a baby. Sure, we might be busy or might not want to be inconvenienced by the task of

> Love even
> when it's
> hard.

helping someone else, but if you really stop and think about it, isn't it more often than not that we are actually afraid of being rejected?

I would have done anything for Winnie, because Winnie would never reject my offer. He would never say no to a cookie or a cuddle, and he would never leave me after I offered him my heart and my home. I felt safe loving Winnie, so how could I learn to feel safe loving the world?

Lina had called me on this during our breakup, telling me, "I don't understand, Leon. If you barely knew me, I could call you in the middle of the night and ask for help, and you would come running. But here I am, asking for you to drive three hours to see my grandmother, and you hesitate."

"It's not that," I lamely replied.

"Then what is it?" she continued. "Why love the strangers and not the person who loves you back?"

"Because maybe one day you won't."

And there you have it, people.

I wish I could say I learned my lesson, and have done all the right things since. But like Bertrand said, relationships take practice, and part of practice is failure.

We don't learn the Way of the Traveler overnight. It took me years to understand that human connection wraps around this world like the plane routes

We are all manifestations of each other.

I so frequently take, connecting communities from one side of the globe to the other. At first, it was about just slowly coming to understand that there was a world outside of myself. The exhaustion on a single mum's face riding to work on the tube, the quiet sadness of a coworker after going through a breakup, the hunched shoulders of a homeless man waiting for change on the corner—it was as though I had never seen these people before. I was so busy thinking about what I needed or what I lacked that I didn't even think about what *they* might need.

Then one day I started to.

After a while, it started to happen naturally.

And it can happen to all of us. We can all get into the practice of kindness.

It starts when you see a tired passenger on the train, and you can't help but say as you get off, "Have a great day!" You can't help but take your recently divorced coworker to lunch, and ask, "Is there anything I can do?" And though you might start by giving that homeless man a dollar, after a while, you can't help but ask his name. Then you begin to get to know him. You learn that he's been on the streets for more than ten years. You find out you once visited his hometown. You discover that he was once a barber, and that he would love to start working again. And then you start looking into barber schools when you're bored at work, and suddenly, you have gone from someone who only thought of themselves to someone who is offering a homeless man you once barely knew the chance to go to barber school.

I've heard it said that if you want to have self-esteem, you need to do estimable acts. Likewise, if you want to help yourself, help someone else.

If I followed Bertrand's theory about practicing the act of giving, then maybe if I continued giving to those I didn't know, I would one day be able to give completely to those I knew best. Just as I had learned to care about the homeless man on the street, I would bring that same level of compassion into my intimate relationships.

We all have to start somewhere.

How Can You Give Winnie Love?

How can you start giving Winnie Love in your life today? Can you bring Winnie Love into your family and intimate relationships? Can you spread Winnie love at work or at school? Can you offer Winnie Love to the strangers you meet every day, offering them your vulnerability whether they accept it or not? Think of three areas where you can start sharing Winnie Love today.

1. _____

_____

_____

_____

_____

2. _____
_____
_____
_____
_____

3. _____
_____
_____
_____
_____

Relationships are a tricky business. They act as microscopes on our flaws and failures, on all our rough edges and difficult behaviors. They illuminate the worst of ourselves, and they inspire us to be better people. The reason they cause so much anxiety, enough that many people have trouble committing to them, is that they ask us to give and be willing to be hurt. They demand that we crack our hearts wide open and share everything with someone who could at any given moment turn their backs forever. But that is also their great promise. Because when that person refuses to walk away, even when we're being our most difficult, they teach us the greatest lesson we can offer one another. They teach us Winnie Love.

Life is about practice, not perfection.

SO DO SOMETHING ABOUT IT

A few years ago, I decided to spend a month in a rural village in Peru. I had signed up with a program that would have me working in an orphanage for a month near Cuzco, in the Sacred Valley. The only problem with the Sacred Valley is that it's nearly 10,000 feet high. When I got off the plane, I couldn't breathe. Literally couldn't breathe. I went to sleep for two days with altitude sickness, but even when I emerged, I still didn't feel right. My stomach was a mess, and my head felt like I was suffering from the world's worst headache. I seriously considered going home, or at least, heading to Lima where I would get to sleep in a nice hotel closer to sea level. I decided I would try out the orphanage for a day, and if I still felt like crap, well, sorry, kids, this chap's got to go.

My apprenticeship included teaching the children English, preparing their food, and in general, doing everything I could to keep them from remembering they were alone in the world. The amazing thing about these kids was, as much as they all wanted a home, they really just wanted to be loved. At the root of every human being is a desire for acceptance.

Back in the 1960s, scientists did an experiment with monkeys to prove the innate need for comfort. The monkeys were given two choices: They could receive food from a metal robot monkey, or they could receive comfort from a robot monkey covered in downy fur. The monkeys all chose the latter, prioritizing comfort over food. Love is a basic need, as strong as any other. We all crave the comfort of the love—the nurturing, the safe space—that all humans are capable of creating for one another. We get to decide—do we want to be the metal monkey, or do we want to be the ones who offer comfort?

The children at the Peruvian orphanage asked for nothing more than my time and attention. In their joy, the desperation of their scenarios was muted. And by the end of the first day, so was my headache.

For the rest of the month, I still battled altitude sickness, but when I was in the presence of those kids, it didn't seem to matter. I wasn't worried about me. I was giving to them. But here's the real secret about giving: Whenever we're giving to someone, we're actually receiving back from them, too. Because here is another scientific fact: Having compassion and empathy changes our neurology. Researchers have recognized that pain-sensitive parts of the brain are activated when we empathize with others who are in pain. We literally feel other people's pain.

I have experienced that level of empathy all over the world—both on the receiving and giving ends. But it is always there, reminding us that, at the end of the day, we are all very much in this together.

Famous traveler St. Augustine supposedly said, "The world is a book, and those who do not travel read only a page." But along the Way of the Traveler, I discovered that if I wasn't willing to give to someone else along my travels, I was reading the wrong book.

In that orphanage in Peru, I learned that I couldn't be

there for those children unless I really listened to what they needed. Since we didn't speak the same language, I needed to listen in a way that I never had before: I needed to listen with my heart.

Through the years, as my travels became less about me and more about the people I met, I found that listening with my heart changed every conversation I had. And it's not that I asked such great questions. I am no Barbara Walters. No, it's just that I stopped thinking about myself long enough to hear what they had to say.

We can all become love.

Do I do this all the time? What do you think? I consistently fail at it. But the heart is also a muscle. Just like Bertrand suggested, I needed to practice listening in order to become better at it. After many years, I am constantly surprised when I am talking to someone, and they say, "Thank you for hearing me."

Because for many years, I didn't hear anyone at all, least of all myself.

It wasn't until I started reaching out to others and hearing about their lives that I began to listen more to that voice within myself. It was through developing empathy for others that I developed empathy for me.

I once heard a story about an elderly woman and her grandson who went to the zoo. The boy had a face covered in freckles. And as he stood in line with many other children, waiting to get his face painted, one of the children turned to him and said, "You've got so many freckles, there's no place to paint!"

Embarrassed, the little boy dropped his head. His grandmother knelt down next to him.

"I love your freckles. When I was a little girl, I always wanted freckles," she said, while tracing her finger across the child's cheek. "Freckles are beautiful."

The boy looked up, "Really?"

"Of course," said the grandmother. "Why, just name me one thing that's prettier than freckles."

The little boy thought for a moment, peered intensely into his grandma's face and softly whispered, "Wrinkles."

It's when I love the wrinkles on another person's face, that I can appreciate my freckles. By having empathy for those in the world who are sick or suffering or just wishing for a better day, I am lifted out of whatever might be marring my own.

How Can You Give Back?

Volunteering can be done no matter where you are, and no matter how little time you have. Pick one day this month, even if it's just for a couple of hours. Decide where you would like to volunteer. You can go online and see how to sign up, or give the organization a call and see when their next information session is. Think of one place you would like to volunteer and then write down their information below. All it takes is one phone call to change your life forever, and maybe someone else's life too.

_____

_____

_____

_____

It's that easy. Start with one day. Remember, our heart is a muscle. We are learning to develop it and shape it so we can one day use it with abandon. But for today, let's just start with that first push-up. With time, you'll find what people have been discovering since the dawn of time, that by giving, we receive. That by listening to others, we are finally heard.

THE LONELY HEARTS CLUB BAND

When the Beatles wrote *Sgt. Pepper's Lonely Hearts Club Band*, they decided to take on alter egos in order to become more musically free. Suddenly, they weren't the Beatles anymore. They had shed their old identities and become someone else. And they were able to be creative in ways they never had been before.

They went from being the world's most popular band to being the world's greatest. And there's no arguing with me on that one. I am an Englishman, after all.

Sometimes we need to shed our old identities in order to really give to those around us. Sometimes we get trapped by our own labels, and are not able to be our best selves because we're too busy being the jealous brother, the selfish daughter, the bad boyfriend.

In Goleman's *Social Intelligence*, he explains what other noted scientists have discovered about kindness: "Although humans inherit a biological bias that permits them to feel anger, jealousy, selfishness and envy, and to be rude, aggressive or violent, they inherit an even stronger biological bias for kindness, compassion, cooperation, love and nurture—especially toward those in need."

Anger, jealousy, and selfishness all serve their purposes. Anger can motivate us toward righteousness, prompting us to stand up for what is right and against what is wrong. Jealousy can show us what we are lacking in our own lives, what dreams we are failing to fulfill. Selfishness can be a form of self-preservation. As they say on airplanes, we need to put our own oxygen mask on first before we can help someone else. All these traits have helped us survive.

> People don't care what you know; they care how you make them feel.

But kindness has also helped us survive. At some point in history, we learned that we had a better chance of survival if we cooperated with one another as a tribe. We learned that, in order to continue the species, we had to mate, and so we connected through love. And we learned that we also needed to nurture the most vulnerable in the tribe, the babies, the elderly, the sick, those in need.

And sometimes we are the ones in need.

Two months after Lina and I broke up, Winston died.

I knew it was coming. I had Winston for twelve years. Over the last few months of his life, he had been getting sicker. I nurtured him the best I could. I tried different medications, and different foods, and even doggy massage (because who doesn't love a massage?), but eventually the time had come. To keep him alive any longer would have been worse than selfish; it would have been cruel.

I called the friends who knew Winston, who had experienced Winnie Love directly from him. We gave him a party; we offered him kindness and compassion, and an insulting amount of dog biscuits, and we said good-bye. One of the last people to leave was Lina.

As she walked out the door, she asked when it would be happening.

I told her I had scheduled the appointment the following morning.

"Call me when you get home," she said. "I'll come over."

Lina and I had spent four years under the wrong title—boyfriend and girlfriend, soul mates, meant to be. The titles had weighed so heavily on our shoulders that we eventually reached the point where we were no longer able to be ourselves. But as she stood at my door that day, I knew what we would always be: friends.

We all have these people in our lives. They are our friends "for always and always and always," as Kipling wrote. They love us even when we don't know how to love ourselves, and they walk us through those dark days, even if we can't always feel them there.

The next morning, I said good-bye to the one friend I had loved more than anyone else, and I watched him leave my life.

I don't even remember the drive home.

I just remember that my heart was shattered in ways I had never experienced, and like a lot of lonely hearts, I called that wonderful, amazing, brilliant beautiful woman who had just recently left my life, and I asked her for help.

As Lina told me during one of those sad days after, "Dogs are like babies. They don't have egos. They just have basic needs. They just need to be fed and kept safe and loved. That's why they love us so purely. And why we are able to love them back."

What collapses your ability to love?

During that time, Lina and I left our egos behind, too.

In *The Soulmate Contract*, authors Caroline Myss and Andrew Harvey write about the idea that our spirits enter into agreements before we even arrive on the planet in order to achieve our destinies. Who am I to say whether this is true or not, but I do believe that we enter into unstated contracts with the people, and even animals, we love. These relationships give us permission—force us, even—to be who we really are, and through the course of their existence, whether for a short period of time or for happily ever after, they help us embrace our truest selves.

I knew that Winnie was one of my soul mates, as was Lina, as she walked me through those dark days, and kept me rooted in those basic needs of being human: making sure I had food, helping me sleep, giving me comfort, offering me her friendship.

The Way of the Traveler brings us back to those basic needs. Because the long, exhausting days on the road don't give us much space to worry about anything else—our only concerns are how we are to be fed, how to be safe, how to love and be loved. Ego is extra baggage. It weighs us down. And it will weigh down any relationship we encounter along the path. During my travels, I have come to recognize that the only way to explore the world is with compassion and cooperation. I have traveled the world, relying on the kindness of strangers, but even more than that, I have gotten to know the world because I have offered it the same kindnesses in turn.

We can go into any situation—whether it is asking for directions in the center of Paris or offering to help our ex—with our boxing gloves on. But the Way of the Traveler is a path of kindness and compassion. That is how we connect to the people we meet along the way. We must walk that adventurous road of cooperation and love. There we will find that it keeps us safe when the world feels broken. Because we realize that a broken heart isn't the most dangerous thing in the world; in fact, it's the natural consequence of love.

How Can You Give to Your Soul Mates?

Lina taught me a powerful lesson that week. She showed me that Winnie Love is alive in all of us. She put aside our past in order to be there for me as a friend. And in turn, we both became better people for it. We became the people we were always meant to be. Who are three of your soul mates? Write down one way you can show Winnie Love for each.

1. _____

_____

_____

_____

2. _____

_____

_____

_____

3. _____

_____

_____

_____

Lina once told me that to love someone is to learn the song in their heart, and then sing it to them whenever they have forgotten it. Because love is like music—it transcends everything we are; it connects us to our unconsciousness; and it taps us into the sacred, no matter where we are or what we are doing. But sometimes, we lose sight of that inner song.

We get trapped in our routines and stop evolving in our relationships. We can't listen to the other person's needs, because we think we already know what they want. And we forget their song, along with our own. We risk becoming lonely hearts, when we could have been soul mates.

Sometimes we have to become someone else in order to become our best selves. Just ask John, Paul, George, and Ringo. It's no coincidence that *Sgt. Pepper's Lonely Hearts Club Band* ends with "A Little Help from My Friends." It is by helping people that we are rescued from loneliness. It is by loving others that we are finally loved.

Love is the great art.

EIGHT

THE WAY
OF THE TRAVELER
STARTS AT HOME

"I long, as does every human being, to be at home wherever I find myself."

—MAYA ANGELOU

I always believed the big dream was out there. I have traveled the whole world, searching for that dream. The great adventure. The major score. I thought home was a boring place filled with the same people and the same chores. But after living out of a backpack for years, I realized that home is where the adventure begins. We can't change the world (or even really enjoy it) until we've created change at home.

But if you're anything like me, then you know that staying home can often be the biggest challenge. The Way of the Traveler delivers us onto many paths, and for me, that path led to the Greek island of Mykonos. If you've never been there before, let me describe it: white sandstone buildings, colorful fishing boats, water as clear as the Dalai Lama's soul, and people, beautiful adventurous people, from all over the world wandering through its antiquated alleys, and lounging on its perfect alabaster beaches.

And people wonder why I travel all the time.

Well, it wasn't so long ago that I ended up on Mykonos because, yet again, I felt like Ishmael. It had become a damp, drizzly November in my soul, and I decided it was high time to get to the sea, or rather, its white, sandy beaches. Because even a consummate traveler needs to take a vacation.

On my first night in Mykonos, I decided to join the island's famous nightlife and see if I could meet some new friends. I put on my best trousers and my loudest T-shirt and went out into the full-moon night. It didn't take long for me to find my people.

When I first started traveling, I spent a lot of my time alone. And maybe that's what I needed at the beginning. But then I started to reach out. I would identify fellow travelers in my midst and invite myself along to whatever adventure they were in the middle of. Most of the time, they were happy for me to join.

I went to a local café and quickly found myself in conversation with two chaps from Nepal, Hari and Paresh. They were making their way across southern Europe, and had stopped in Mykonos before heading on to Spain. Earlier in the day, they had met two French travelers who were on a similar course. Noemie and Gaelle worked together at a marketing firm in Paris. After they arrived, we ended up meeting up with a duo from Hungary, Miki and Olga, sib- lings on vacation with their parents. They had managed to get away for the night and were hoping to go dancing.

Engage your heart, and you will engage the world.

Together, our motley crew of international travelers made its way across the island. We ate and danced and drank, and as the night turned to dawn, we made our way into the Aegean Sea. Hari and I ended up floating away from the others as we spoke. Like how my trip to Nepal had inspired my own life of adventure, Hari had gone to London as a teen and been similarly inspired to travel the globe.

Hari told me, "I grew up thinking I would never leave Ne- pal. And then I got into this school; it was for boys from better families. And all these opportunities came up—like going to London, like seeing the world."

As he explained, "For a long time, I would be Hari at home—the boy from the village. And then I would be Hari in the world—educated, worldly. But I stopped feeling at home in either place."

I used to be two Leons, also. The Leon who went to Myko- nos and met fascinating people and experienced life to its fullest, and the Leon who came home and lived a lie. Did the right things. Said the right things. Wore the right things. But I wasn't "me" in either place—I was living half-lives in both because I hadn't learned who either of those people really were. In many ways, with each trip, I am still learning, and likewise, the man who is happy on the road has become the same man who is happy at home.

Hari told me how he finally met the person who changed everything.

"Paresh and I met at university," he told me. "He was from one of those better families, and he had the confidence where he could go anywhere and feel at home. He told me that he realized that we were all the same. Me, from my village, and he, from his fancy neighborhood. And suddenly, I began to see that, too."

We drifted out, farther from the group, as Hari continued, "I guess seeing the world has really shown me that. All different countries, different cultures. Yet we are not so different. And then suddenly, when I started returning home, I didn't feel so different there, either."

I understood. It took me seeing the world to finally feel at home. It's a lesson I have realized I might need to learn more than once. The Way of the Traveler is not about perfection; it's about evolution. It's about learning a lesson and then realizing, sometimes the next day, sometimes many years later, that you need to learn the lesson again.

I realized then that I didn't have to go to Mykonos to feel connected. Because wherever I go, whether to Mykonos or the

Starbucks up the street from my house, the opportunities for learning and adventure are there as long as I am willing to listen. As long as I am willing to change.

THE VISION QUEST

It was only a few thousand years ago that most people on this beautiful blue planet of ours were nomads. They would travel the plains or mountains or tundra, hunting for food and shelter. They would also go in search of themselves. Some indigenous people believed that in order to find this true self, one had to go on a vision quest in order to meet their spirit. They would embark on treacherous journeys, not only to test their prowess in the wild, but also to determine what their spiritual destiny would be.

Miracles are born of intuition.

When I returned to Los Angeles after my stay in Mykonos, it was to a different life. Winston was gone. Lina was gone. I was once again on my own. The nomad had returned.

Barely a week had passed when my phone rang.

"Let's go for a hike," Steve suggested.

And so Steve and I set off on our greatest adventure yet: We drove to Palmdale.

Palmdale is a small city about forty miles north of Los Angeles. It was rumored to have a good barbecue place and Steve loved barbecue. We drove up through the Angeles National Forest, along a winding and wooded road through the wilderness on the outskirts of LA.

The life I had once planned was gone, but in its place was the life I was always meant to lead. I had become an author, I was hosting my own TV show, and I was traveling the country, speaking to young people about their limitless potential. More often than not, those young people were becoming accidental teachers in my life, too. I was connecting with the world in ways I had always dreamed, and I was finally living that dream. Though my heart had been shaken to its core, my spirit knew I was exactly where I was supposed to be.

Steve and I pulled off the road for a hike, making our way up to the top of Mount Baldy, which stands over the northern part of Los Angeles like a protective mother. Many people ask why I have chosen LA as my home, and my answer is simple: From it, I have access to both wild nature and wild city. As we moved along the well-worn path, leading up the mountain, the air began to cool, clearing my mind as only mountain air can do.

Henry David Thoreau once wrote that, "We need the tonic of wildness."

Among the trees and the brush, I began to feel myself healed in ways that even the warmest waters of the Aegean could not provide. After a while, I realized I was lagging behind Steve, as he quickly made his ascent. I could see Los Angeles peeking out from behind the cliff's edge, and I could feel my spirit settle into an easy peace.

I stopped for a moment to rest, and that is when I saw it. A family of deer shared my path just up ahead. They also stopped. The large buck stood in front of his doe and their fawn. There was no intimidation in the buck's stance. He looked at me as though I was just another fellow traveler, both of us enjoying the morning air.

I nodded to the deer family, and I might be crazy, but the buck seemed to nod back.

Then they bounded up the mountainside and out of view, and I knew then, perhaps more than in any other moment, that I did not need to look far for adventure. Because the universe's greatest magic tricks often reside in our own backyards.

I met Steve at the top of Mount Baldy, where we stood overlooking the city I had chosen to call home. My vision quest hadn't taken place along some back road of a Southeast Asian town. No Ecuadorian jungles were required. In fact, we didn't even have to drive to another state.

It is a wonderful life.

No, my quest came in the easy camaraderie of friendship, along the quiet and empty roads of my adopted hometown, watching hawks fly overhead, much like that eagle in Nepal. Only this time, the hawks were reminding me that I didn't have to go far to still be able to soar high.

"So what are you going to do now?" Steve asked me.

Singer Sam Smith shared in a Grammy acceptance speech,

"It's only when I started to be myself that the music started to flow and the people started to listen."

I thought about sharing this quote with Steve, but I already knew he'd make fun of me.

"I'm going to be myself," I told him.

This is the ultimate destination of the Way of the Traveler. It is the treasure that Santiago ultimately finds buried beneath the tree in his own backyard. It is the life that waits for us if we're willing to let go of the one that was planned for us, and instead embrace the one we are meant to live.

The Way of the Traveler magnifies our dreams and our failures. It allows us to connect with others and shows where we have failed to connect, both with the people we love most and with the strangers around us. It leads us into love and illuminates our fears. It pulls us out of ourselves and into the deepest journeys of our lives.

The Way of the Traveler is right in front of you. It is in your backyard as much as it is in mine. As much as it was in Santiago's. But we have to be the ones to seek that adventure. We have to be willing to go out on that vision quest in order to find our spiritual destiny. But as I learned during Steve's visit, I didn't need to go far.

What Is Your Vision Quest?

What adventure can you take today to connect with that powerful spirit inside? Should you go to a local art museum? A hike in nature? A trip to the beach? List three Vision Quests you can take in your city. Then set some time aside for yourself, invite a friend if you wish, and take a day to explore the world around you.

1. _____

_____

_____

2. _____

_____

_____

3. _____

_____

_____

THE HERO'S JOURNEY

Like with *The Alchemist*, I stumbled upon Joseph Campbell's *The Hero with a Thousand Faces* without really knowing what it was about. At first, it felt too heady for me—so much transformation, so much transcendence—but then I came upon this quote, "Perhaps some of us have to go through dark and devious ways before we can find the river of peace or the highroad to the soul's destination."

Have you ever seen the very first *Star Wars* movie (*Episode*

IV: A New Hope)? Even of the legions who have, many don't know that Luke Skywalker's journey was actually influenced by the writings of Joseph Campbell. Luke had to engage with the dark side before he could find his rightful place among the Jedi knights. Much like Louise's story of the wolves, we have to walk through the sorrow in order to appreciate the joy. That is the quest for all of us, as we are the heroes of our own lives.

But our journey doesn't require lightsabers or Ewoks, although both of those things would be cool. No, our journey requires that we go to those deep, dark places within. That is why the Way of the Traveler can be lived without ever leaving one's city. In fact, I have found that some of the greatest adventures can take place close to home.

> We are all emotionally delicate creatures.

After my vision quest with Steve, I knew that it was time again to go within myself, because like Joseph Campbell's hero, the real journey still lay within. And guess what? I didn't need to go anywhere to get there.

The only tools I needed were a sense of wonder and the desire to leave my comfort zone. This time, it wasn't about seeing the world, but about changing how I saw the world. And how I saw myself.

My next big adventure was probably the most terrifying of them all.

I had my dream job. I was single. Winston was gone. My house was empty, and I decided to stay put. In fact, as I write this, I have been on that adventure for six months. And sometimes walking to the kitchen in the morning can be the most daring trip I have ever taken. Because I am learning to be happy at home, but even beyond that, I am learning to be happy alone.

In 1845, Henry David Thoreau left society to build his own house in the woods. There, he grew his own food and lived a life of simplicity in the middle of rural Massachusetts. Thoreau believed that we easily lose ourselves through the distractions of ordinary life. Through his solitude, he realized, "I went to the woods because I wished to live deliberately, to front only the essential facts of life, and see if I could not learn what it had to teach, and not, when I came to die, discover that I had not lived. I did not wish to live what was not life, living is so dear; nor did I wish to practice resignation, unless it was quite necessary. I wanted to live deep and suck out all the marrow of life."

It's easy to suck out the marrow of life when you're out on the road. But coming home is a different experience. Whether your journeys have taken you to far-flung places or into the deeper parts of your soul, the biggest challenge is how to bring those lessons home. It is there that we need to learn to live deliberately every day, and suck out the marrow of life both during the most adventurous times, and the most mundane.

The Way of the Traveler is ultimately creating that adventure everywhere you go. It is about waking up with the attitude of a child—curious to see the world as though for the first time, and learn from it. And sometimes all it takes are the simplest shifts to create the most powerful transformations. Like the butterfly effect, we find we don't need to go to the ends of the world to seek enlightenment; we just have to make small, subtle changes.

Because I have also learned—the hard way—that I will never be able to be someone's partner until I am comfortable with that man in the mirror. I may have learned to jump at opportunity. I may have learned to dream the big dream. I may even have learned how to experience and share joy with every man, woman, and dog on this planet—specifically, the island of Mykonos—but I won't experience love, at least not the kind that will last, unless I am willing to do the work on myself, to find time to meditate, to journal, to listen to that spirit guiding me gently inside, and through it all, to create a faith big enough to contain my fears.

Embrace your own brilliance.

That life is waiting for us, right around the corner. The next job. The next great love. The next moment of joy. The next moment of teaching. But until we can be okay with the still of the morning or the quiet of the night, we will never be able to appreciate all the treasures around us and all the treasures to come. This is the hero's journey, and we are all on it.

In order to find that river of peace, we must remove those final branches blocking our path. We must see where in our lives we still have work to do. Is it our job? Is it our love life?

Is it our fears, which still block us from finding the peace that others, like Hari from Nepal, have been able to obtain?

So let's go back to Mykonos for a moment. Let's pick up where Hari and I left off, floating in the sea.

After we got out of the water, I asked Hari, "Are you as happy at home as you are when you're traveling?"

Hari smiled, "Happier."

"How?" I asked.

"Because I keep this world with me," he shared. "I see it from afar, but more than that, I see it in me."

Me too, brother. Me. We.

How Can You Remove the Last Branches?

Look at your life as it is right now. Is there something blocking you from peace? Is it financial fear? Is it emotional stress? What stops you today from being at ease with what you have and who you are and what are you going to do about it? Do you need to call a creditor? Do you need to call your mum? Write down two things that you can do today to remove those dead branches.

1. _____
_____
_____
_____
_____

2. _____

_____

_____

_____

_____

We don't need to go anywhere to find the solutions to our troubles. In the "hero's journey" (as Campbell describes), the hero reaches transformation with the aid of mentors and helpers. He cannot do it alone. And neither can we. We need to find the Steves in our lives, and the Haris, the people who can share with us the truths we need to hear.

Who can help you? Maybe it's a friend, or a parent, or maybe it's a professional. Maybe its time you found a financial advisor or a therapist. Maybe it's time you confronted an addiction or reached out to a local community group for help. Maybe it's as easy as joining a book club or starting a club focused on a hobby or interest. How can you create a tribe of people who will help you reach your goals, who will help guide you through the thickets and back to the deepest river of them all: home?

THE PASSION STARTS NOW

Once, I had a dream to cross the world on the kindness of strangers. It was a ridiculous dream. Some might have said it was impossible.

But I did it. I went across the globe. I turned strangers into friends. I learned to love in ways I never thought possible. And I freed myself from the stories and belief systems and limitations that had held me back from living the purest, most authentic adventure, the one we all will discover when we are finally able to be ourselves.

> You will know your passion by what fulfills your soul.

But what many people forget, myself included, is that it took me a decade to get there. A decade between when I first had that big dream to cross the world on the kindness of strangers, and when I made it happen. A lot happened between those two points—different jobs, different cities, different homes, different girlfriends—but one thing didn't change, my passion for the dream.

How Can You Make Your Big Dream Come True?

The Way of the Traveler will open your heart in ways you never thought possible. It will open your eyes to worlds beyond. Ultimately, it will open your spirit up to who you are and who you are to become. And it all starts with that big, ridiculous, impossible dream. Remember that one? You wrote it down on pages 27–28 of this book. Well, now it's time to return to it. Every big dream demands a big plan. Now, it's time to start developing yours. What can you do today to make your dream come true? What does that plan look like, and how can you go about achieving it?

_____

_____

_____

_____

_____

_____

_____

_____

_____

_____

So, let's go back to Mykonos, one last time.

As our little tribe headed back into town, just as the sun began to rise. I told Hari that, on one of his next trips, he should come to Los Angeles.

Live your adventure NOW.

"Yes," he replied. "That would be a dream."

And now it's time to decide where *you* will go. If a young man from a small Nepalese town can travel the world, certainly we are all capable of living out our great dreams.

The Way of the Traveler is the road map to those dreams. It illuminates our true purpose that has been blocked by our fears and insecurities, some instilled by others, some sadly created on our own. And along its path, we learn to fully live. We wake up every day with an energy we didn't know possible. We take our moment to meditate, to go for a walk, to head to the gym, to breathe in the morning air as though an eagle is forever flying overhead, reminding us of our own ability to soar.

And then that big, ridiculous dream doesn't seem so impossible anymore.

I hope by now you have become the hero on your journey, that you have found your village, embraced risk, gotten out of your own way, and learned to care for the world with the greatest of Winnie Love.

I hope you have learned to identify the accidental teachers in your life—the people who guide us, illuminating our truths and fears, and look at us with the complete and utter confidence that we have longed for our whole lives. And I hope you get to become an accidental teacher yourself, passing along inspiration, so that you, too, can look at someone you love and sing their song, even

I see who you are!

when—*especially* when—they have forgotten how to sing it. And through that shared song, you will learn to share your passion, and your trust. You will learn to share your intimacy.

So put your hand on your heart, and feel what courses inside you. Remember that, above all, we are mortal. We only get one fleeting chance at this business called life, and we only get one chance to share this life with others. Go out and ask that world to dance. Dance madly. Dance like you believe in impossible dreams. And you'll soon find that the more you commit to that dream, the more possible it becomes.

And then lastly, share that passion with others. I know that's my next big dream. It's no longer about Leon. Leon and I are good. It's about Me. We. It's about discovering new lands together.

Like Aardash said, "We walk now." And so we walk.

THE WAY
OF THE TRAVELER
HAS JUST BEGUN

"To touch the soul of another human being is to walk on holy ground."

—STEPHEN COVEY

Oh, no. We're not done yet. In fact, the Way of the Traveler has now just begun for you. I have read enough books like this to know how easy it is to set them down and then forget all the promises you made to yourself while reading it. Maybe you did the written activities and really feel you have already started on the Way of the Traveler.

Or maybe your book looks a bit less full.

Either way, I am going to ask that you now go back. You can read the book again if you want (I'll be very impressed), but more importantly, I want you to read what you have written. I want you to turn those exercises into your road map. Refer to them as you make new choices in your life, add to them as you discover new things, use them everyday to center you in the present moment, and in the life you were meant to lead.

Because the Way of the Traveler doesn't live in a book. It lives in our everyday lives, in our relationships, in the decisions we make about who we are and who we want to be.

But our journey does not have to end here. In fact, if you're interested, our journey together will have just begun. Because I have another adventure for you. And this time, it's far away from the page, and in the real world, together.

As is by now very obvious, travel has changed my life. It has defined who I am, and I want to share these experiences with you. Yes, *you*. That is my next big dream.

Like my experience in India, I am offering similar expeditions called, you guessed it, the Way of the Traveler. They are epic adventures in various locations around the world. They are about finding your spiritual destiny. They are about embracing your big dream. They are about discovering that great treasure within.

And they are about seeing the world as you have never seen it before.

That's right. Together, we will walk the Way of the Traveler. We will meet in foreign lands. Maybe we'll even meet in your backyard, but I will do my best to show you what travel can bring into your life, and how you can then take those lessons home and share them with others.

Even if we don't journey together, I hope this book inspires your own adventure. Whether it's to the museum in your hometown or to that Nepalese hillside where the eagles are waiting to greet you, I hope you use this book as your diving board into the world around you, into the relationships in your life today, and on to that adventurous road to your best life. I look forward to meeting you there.

I promise
If you keep
Searching
For everything
Beautiful
In this world

You will
Eventually
Become it.
—TYLER KENT WHITE

ACKNOWLEDGMENTS

I am tremendously grateful to all the people who helped turn this project into a reality. First, to my parents, who always believed in me and who showed me just how much one can love another human being.

To my three brothers, George, Con, and Nick. We may be separated by thousands of miles but nothing will ever break the bonds of love I feel for you.

Isabella, Michael, George, John-Michael, Philip and Daisy—I hope this book reminds you that we are always free to create wonderful lives. I love you all.

Andrea and the team at Readers Digest, your faith inspired this dream. Kristen, without your brilliance this book wouldn't have happened. I appreciate you and your magic editing sprinkles more than you know. Thank you.

Naasih, thank you for enabling me to see with my heart. Graham and Kerry, thanks for reminding me to write from my soul—and not from my head! Alfa, your friendship and wisdom helped make this book what it is.

Ramchandra, words cannot express the impact you have

had on my life, and how the effects of your knowledge continue to touch new lives.

Last but not least, I want to thank Winston for teaching me how to love. You changed my life in more ways than you will ever know. I carry your memory with me, always.

ABOUT THE AUTHOR

Leon Logothetis is a global adventurer, motivational speaker, and philanthropist. It wasn't always that way. He used to be a broker in the city of London, where he felt uninspired and chronically depressed. He gave it all up for a life on the road. This radical life change was brought about by the inspirational movie *The Motorcycle Diaries*.

The days of living and working behind his "slab of wood" (or desk to the layman) are well and truly over.

Leon has visited more than ninety countries and traveled to every continent. Among his adventures:

- He teamed up with First Book and drove a car from London to Mongolia, raising money to buy 10,000 books for underprivileged children in America.

- He drove a vintage London taxi across America, giving free cab rides to the needy, and working with Class-wish to bring hope back to the schools of America.

- He crossed America, the United Kingdom, and Europe on just five dollars, five pounds, and five euros a day, respectively, chronicling these trips on the TV series *Amazing Adventures of a Nobody*, which was broadcast across the world by National Geographic International, and in a book of the same name.

- He circumnavigated the globe on his vintage yellow motorbike Kindness One, while relying on the kindness of strangers. Along the way, he gave life-changing gifts to unsuspecting Good Samaritans, telling their stories on the TV series *The Kindness Diaries,* and in a book of the same name.

In addition, Leon has documented his travels for numerous media outlets, including *Good Morning America,* the *Los Angeles Times,* the *San Francisco Chronicle, Outside, Good, Psychology Today,* and the *New York Times.* The founder of the Human Interaction Project (HIP), he lives in Los Angeles, California. He also offers seminars and courses in the Way of the Traveler. For additional information, please visit WayoftheTraveler.com.

INDEX